Wisdom From The Wild

Patrick J. Diggs

Foreword By: Rev. Roosevelt Baugh

Published by BLI Publishing, Dallas, TX.

Printed though Createspace.

Printed in the United States of America.

ISBN: 0692497250
ISBN-13: 978-0692497258

DEDICATION

In loving memory of my nephew Michael Lamont Rogers.

January 1, 1979- September 25, 2014

My friend and apprentice who passed of congestive heart failure.

TABLE OF CONTENTS

ACKNOWLEDGMENTS

Christopher Smith, Executive Pastor of Trinity Harvest Church: You told me of a series they were doing at your church, Trinity Harvest Church, Pastor Ray Taylor, Senior Pastor, called *Out of the Wild* that gave birth to the idea of this book. He is the Executive Pastor of Trinity Harvest.

New Fellowship Church of Fort Worth: Thank you for allowing me to preach Wisdom from the wild to you for a month as we learned about obedience.

To my children: Patrick Jordan, Britney Danielle, Raven Monet, for supporting your dad in everything he does without reservation.

To my wife: Thank you. You are my personal cheerleader and best friend. I love you.

To God: Thank you for giving me the insight and energy to investigate the behavioral traits of your animals in order to learn how to be more obedient to Christ.

FOREWORD

One of my life's rare coveted delights and privileges has been to witness the sustained growth of a human personality. The growth and maturing spiritually of a mind and soul is one of God's most beautiful accomplishments and delightful things to witness. That, I have been privileged to see in the life of the author of this book.

I first came to know him some 10 years ago. I have seen him "study to show himself approved unto God, a workman that need not to be ashamed, rightly dividing the word of truth." From his ministry has come the fruitful development of a vibrant congregation known as the New Fellowship Church. Patrick James Diggs (fondly called P.J.) is a gifted, energetic preacher, always scriptural, clearly outlined, convicting and encouraging.

This book has been conceived as having two types of content---obedience and disobedience. It is my hope and prayer that the reader will be encouraged to develop a deeper and stronger relationship with God. This is a must read book! I am very grateful for being given the opportunity and privilege of writing this foreword.

I am also happy to say that the author of this book is my "Beloved son-in-law" in whom I am well pleased.

Rev. Roosevelt Baugh
Pastor, St. Mark Cumberland Presbyterian Church, Fort Worth, TX.

INTRODUCTION

"I do solemnly swear (or affirm) that I will support and defend the Constitution of the United States against all enemies, foreign and domestic; that I will bear true faith and allegiance to the same; and that I will obey the orders of the President of the United States and the orders of the officers appointed over me, according to regulations and the Uniform Code of Military Justice."

When one enlists in the United States military, they take this solemn oath. Enlistees are taught to obey, immediately and without question, orders from their superiors from day-one of boot camp. These are men and women who, because of a sense of duty and maybe even a higher calling, voluntarily put their lives on the line to defend the United States of America. Some feel it is a privilege to fight for the freedom of American citizenship and the right to live in the U.S. without threat of terroristic attacks. Others may feel a sense of obligation because they may have had a family member serve. Whatever it is they take this oath with certainty that they are enlisted in the military until they retire or are discharged.

That's how answering the call of God on your life seems. Many feel they are called, personally by God, to follow Him without question and without fail; while others may feel a sense of obligation because they grew up going to church and it's all that they know. Still there are some who connect with God later in life and that connection drives them to want to reach and teach others who are lost in the world. If and when you hear a higher calling on your life, as those in the military, to serve in the Kingdom of God you should be able and ready to take a similar oath to God. Your fight for the truth of the living word of God should ignite a fire within you to put your life on the line for the sake of preserving another's life, by telling them the Gospel of God. You must be willing, sometimes at all cost, to stand on the word of God, even when it's all that you have, despite oppression, rejection, and even losing those who said they would never turn their backs on you. An individual who responds to the life of others in this manner is one whose life is guided by the greatness and wisdom from God Almighty.

Today, millions of people are on a search for this wisdom, but fall short because they lack the obedience and discipline of the higher calling. But, despite that not being their best or strongest asset, I assure you that if you desire to have a strong relationship with God then being steadfast is essential to your journey. This ongoing search for wisdom is actually a search for God. In fact, inner happiness and fulfillment, in my opinion, only comes when man attains this wisdom. Wisdom is discovered and only enjoyed by those who are diligently determined to find it. Wisdom cannot be discovered by the casual observer. When you are really engaged with your life's calling, whether in the workplace, social world, or through your worship experience, you'll have to rely on something that is caught and not taught.

Reading this book in its entirety will help you become someone who is looking for the answer to the lifelong question:

How do I find happiness and fulfillment?

Well, I don't have all the answers but as one who currently enjoys a life of fulfillment on an admirable level, I can say it was found through living my life in obedience to God, the Creator. I am not saying it was an easy journey because there were times in my journey as a pastor in which I wanted to give it all up just to go fishing and to have a piece of mind. Ministry is challenging but being in obedience with God make all the challenges melt away because I have trained myself to see God and understand where

God is taking me, New Fellowship and the people I am led to teach and bless. I share the thoughts of George Macdonald who said, *"Doing the will of God leaves me no time for disputing about His plans."*

OBEDIENCE is not a word we hear discussed much in our society because rebellion is the hottest and most trending thing. We must rebel against the government. Rebel against what we are taught. Heck, if you aren't rebelling then you are socially an outcast. Still, the traits of disobedience have been a problem from the inception of life in the Garden of Eden. I wonder how the initial fall of man would have happened during our times and if we could conceive the consequences of it. Just think about it.

Adam and Eve, probably wouldn't even be Adam and Eve. They might have been Adam and Steve or Eve and Amanda. Cell phone videos and pictures would have filled our timelines and social media beefs would hit the news stations all over the world. The headlines would read, *"Garden Couple Eat Fruit and Both Deny Their Part In It."* God would be the judge but because we are such an opinionated society His verdict would be skewed because of the courts of public opinion. Satan wouldn't even be on trial because he would be the defense attorney for Eve. She would be victimized as an oppressed woman who was forced to live in the shadows of Adam. Infidelity would be exposed. I also imagine that the American Civil Liberties Union would immediately file suit against God in defense of Eve and her husband Adam citing illegal eviction.

"And after all," we would be told, "this alleged sinful act was performed in the privacy of the garden, and by two consenting adults."

But most of all we would be told that the crime (if indeed there was one) and the punishment were totally out of proportion. Could God really be serious in what this account claims to report? Because of a mere bite of some 'forbidden fruit' the man and woman are evicted from the Garden and will suffer a lifetime of consequence? And more than this, that due to this one act the whole world and ALL mankind continue to suffer the evils that continuously surround us?

Today, pure chaos and drama would ensue because we live a very free spirited life in which we do not want to be held responsible for our acts against God.

For those who do not take the Bible seriously they will have little difficulty with my illustration because they simply write off the third chapter of Genesis as a myth. To them it is merely a symbolic story that endeavors to account for things as they are. They see the details of the fall of Adam and Eve and think that there are no problems, for the so-called fall is not fact, but fiction. They also see the so called oppression of both Adam and Eve by a controlling God who wanted things to go His way or the highway. It saddens me when I hear conversations about Adam and Eve and the initial fall of mankind being uttered from the mouths of nonbelievers as something to NOT believe. I assume that the world got to them and convinced them that neither the story of the fall is true nor is the Bible, if you want to take it a step further.

But, for those who know this story to be true indeed, I know there are several serious questions that arise when pastors across the country and world share this biblical fact:

- Why must Adam assume primary respons ibility when Eve is the principle character of disobedience in the narrative?

- Why did God act so harshly towards then both when Eve was the instigator?
- Why didn't Adam reject Eve's request to partake in the forbidden meal, especially when he knew God's order?

I have heard so many questions but they usually center around these three questions. Believers and nonbelievers alike want to know why all of the subsequent events happened from one singular event.

My only response is when your kids don't do what you tell them to do, how do you respond? Of course, there are some who say they talk to their kids while others say they are disciplined a little more harshly, depending on the "crime." And that's when I let them know that regardless of what their child does or the parent's preferred response, once the child disobeys they are disciplined. God simply disciplined Adam. Eve was a victim of circumstance because she was made from Adam. She was not God's direct child, as many would have you to think. She was made from Adam, who was God's crown and glory. Eve was, from a law perspective, an accessory.

Let's breakdown the thought process a little more why God responded so harshly. First, you must know that God is a God of order. In 1 Corinthians 14:33 King James Version (KJV) it reads, *"For God is not the author of confusion, but of peace, as in all churches of the saints."* That simply means, the way He creates it and what He created it for must remain true. No deviation. No additives. Nothing more than what it was instructed to do when it was made. Unfortunately, over the years, man has removed himself from that simple instruction.

So let's look at some details why disobedience is intolerable to God. In Genesis, chapters 1 and 2, we read of a perfect creation in which everything God created was given His approval which is 'good':

> 10 *And God called the dry land Earth; and the gathering together of the waters called He Seas: and God saw that it was good.*
> 12 *And the earth brought forth grass, and herb yielding seed after his kind, and the tree yielding fruit, whose seed was in itself, after his kind: and God saw that it was good.*
> 18 *And to rule over the day and over the night, and to divide the light from the darkness: and God saw that it was good.*

> [21] *And God created great whales, and every living creature that moveth, which the waters brought forth abundantly, after their kind, and every winged fowl after his kind: and God saw that it was good.*

You see, God took His time when He created the world that we live in today. He made sure that everything on this planet was created for a specific purpose. He made sure that everything had a mate, male and female. There was nothing about God's design that was flawed. He even made two sets of people. Ah, yes. Many of you may not know that God made others before He made Adam. In Gen. 1:26-27 it reads, *"And God said, Let us make man in our image, after our likeness: and let them have dominion over the fish of the sea, and over the fowl of the air, and over the cattle, and over all the earth, and over every creeping thing that creepeth upon the earth. So God created man in his own image, in the image of God created he him; male and female created he them."*

I'll let that sink in for a minute.

God made other people before He made His man, Adam, who is the father of the nation of Israel. This is why God hates disobedience because to Him it is a slap in the face. Kind of like when your child blatantly disobeys you after you've done everything for him or her. So as we look into the second chapter of Genesis we see where God made Adam (Gen. 2:7) to be ruler over the Garden of Eden. God specifically created a man just for Him. And because He didn't want Adam to be alone He put Adam to sleep and created Eve from his rib (Gen. 2:20-22).

Do you understand how special Adam was to God? God created Him differently from the others. He created a special place for him and then gave him dominion to name everything. When He saw that Adam was alone He made Eve for him. God did everything for Adam. Adam didn't want for anything. He didn't even want the forbidden fruit until it was brought to his attention, and then reminded that he could not have it.

But I digress, for the moment, to show you how Adams' direct disobedience caused sin to enter into the world. In chapter 4 of Genesis, we read about jealousy and murder (this is the story of Cain and Abel). In the following chapters mankind goes from bad to worse. Not only were we disobedient, we were hateful and wanted to be God.

What happened? How did this happen? Why did God let this happen?

Genesis 3 answers this question. Disobedience.

Yes. It is just that simple. Disobedience to God is how we ended up living in a world of sin. Remember when God kicked Satan out of the heavens, not only did Satan remove a third of the heavenly host, he also was given dominion of the earth. Satan didn't burst hell wide open as some may think. He was cast out of heaven and fell to earth. Where he rules. Don't believe me read Job 1:7 it reads, *"And the Lord said unto Satan, Whence comest thou? Then Satan answered the Lord, and said, From going to and fro in the earth, and from walking up and down in it."*

So, we were placed into Satan's territory for our disobedience. And it continues to get worst. We see how God uses Moses to bring His chosen people, the Israelites, out of the bondage they were in, in Egypt in the book of Exodus. He gave Moses the heart to take them into the promised life of abundance in the Promised Land, the land of milk and honey, but we know it as Canaan. Although the trip from Egypt took the Israelites through the parted Red Sea, where Pharaoh and his entire army were destroyed, and into the wilderness took 40 years, the transformation seemed to take a lifetime for many. I am not sure if it's an unfortunate situation but some of the Israelites who were led out of captivity never experienced the spiritual makeover that God had for them because of their lack of obedience.

Throughout the Old Testament, there are countless stories of disobedience. Even to the point where God cuts off the northern tribes of Israel. Their refusal to not worship false idols or keep the high holy days sent them into dire straits. That's why the nation of Israel needed a Savior because God truly wanted to destroy Israel but He promised Abraham that his seed would be the chosen people of God.

Jesus told us that He came to give life abundantly (John 10:10). But that abundant life cannot be attained if you choose to feed an appetite of rebellion. The residue that was embedded in Egypt can be seen lingering throughout the pages of biblical history and its sting has ultimately infected Israel. We have gone, at times, so far from God that we have become like the other nations. We refuse to harken to what the Most High is telling us when He says to follow the commandments and to keep His laws and statutes, even to this day. It is your ability to live a life of effective obedience that is worthy of being built on the foundation of God's orders!

Don't ignore the wisdoms on the winding roads of life or you might end up in the wilderness. Eventually, it will become a residence when you were only supposed to go there temporarily, to find rest and to hear from God. Your obedience begins the moment you take the oath to be obedient to God!

If you are struggling with having a disciplined life with uncontested order, then this book is for you. If chaos is your bunkmate and misfortune constantly knocks at your door, then you might benefit from learning more about why and what it means to walk in obedience with God. It does not mean there will be no more mishaps or tests, but you will have an appreciation for His divine order and the wisdom to navigate your life through it. If you really want to find contentment while pleasing God, then your life has to be surrendered over to the Kingdom of God and sacrificed for His service.

As you move through the chapters of this book I want you to remember this Oath…

I do solemnly affirm that I WILL support and defend the message of the Cross against all evil forces and principalities foreign and domestic. I WILL bear fruit from the Word of God and obey the orders of Jehovah God and the spiritual leaders appointed over me according to the precepts found in his Word.

~Your blessing is behind your obedience.

CHAPTER | ONE

GOD'S CLIMAX

John 14:15, "If you love me, you will keep my commandments."

The Day of Disobedience

This chapter is vital because it explains the world and society as we observe it today. It informs us of the strategies of Satan in tempting man. It explains the reason for the New Testament passages that restrict women from assuming leadership roles in the church. It challenges us to consider whether or not we will continue to 'fall' as Adam and Eve did or to take a stand to serve God unconditionally. It also depicts the entrance of sin into the human race and the severity of the consequences of man's disobedience.

However, beyond man's sinfulness and the penalties it demands, there is the revelation of God's amazing grace. God wants His chosen people to diligently seek Him and to trust Him above all, including their simplest understanding. God sent Jesus to be a beacon as a way to come back into His holy presence because the thought is sin is disgusting to God. I know many times you have heard that God loves the sinner despite the sin but I am here to let you know that is a far past due preconceived notion that has kept our people living in sin.

In the article by Jared Moore he shared a sermon from David Platt entitled "God Hates the Sin AND Hates the Sinner AND Loves the Sinner." This powerful piece argued that God hates the sin and hates the sinner and loves the sinner. But the scripture clearly teaches both. Reject the cliche' that God only "hates the sin and loves the sinner." Our sins cannot be separated from us. Jesus didn't just die for my sins; He died for me! He referenced several scriptures such as:

> *Psalm 5:5-6 which reads, "The foolish shall not stand in thy sight: thou hatest all workers of iniquity. 6 Thou shalt destroy them that speak leasing: the LORD will abhor the bloody and deceitful man."*
> *Psalms 11:5 says, "The Lord tests the righteous, But the wicked and the one who loves violence His soul hates."*

I can go on and on because there are so many scriptures that warn us to avoid sin because it leads to destruction when we don't repent and turn away from sin. God wants us to live a life that is covered by Him through Christ Jesus. God promised us a Savior through whom the whole tragic event, when sin entered into the world, will turn into triumph and salvation. God's salvation was written with you in mind. It was written to let you know that you can repent and turn from your sin by living a life of obedience. Obedience is not easy but it is surely worth it because you will be able to connect with God on a personal and intimate level.

I can honestly say that through my life I have learned how to hear wisdom in the things most men ignore and I have zeal to share God's wisdom with whomever will listen. I share with you Proverbs 12:15, *"A wise man listens to advice but a fool listens to his own words."*

I know this… in order to experience this grace that is offered, you mustn't overlook the wisdom God gives you that will lead you to walking obediently with the living Word. Additionally, you must take heed to the behavioral traits of animal life. Yes, there is a word of wisdom that can be seen and learned from wildlife. God covered Adam's and Eve's "fault" with the skin of an animal, cast them out of the Garden and left them to work their way back to the fellowship they once effortlessly had.

You can look at this disobedience as the nail in the coffin but I look at it as a roadmap back to salvation. God put Adam and Eve into the wilderness so that we could benefit from seeing a loving God, through the years, who continues to give His all to a people who do not listen and harken to the wisdom that He gives us every second of our lives.

Thank you Jesus that He still loves us enough to teach us and reach us where we are!

Why is Wildlife So Important to God?

In the first chapter of Genesis, God makes sure that He created animals first. They were here before man and God called them good. Every beast, creeping thing, foul of the air, fish of the sea, and creatures we may have never seen was made by God and was called good by God. Think about that for a second. In those scriptures God points to them and calls them good. That means there was purpose for everything God created before He ever created man. Animals gave God utter and complete obedience. Whatever their purpose was, they obeyed without question. You have to be confident in knowing that kind of constant obedience to God is possible to attain.

But how much time elapsed between the creation of animals and mankind? If you use biblical chronological interpretation, you find out that a day with God is "like" a thousand years (2 Peters 3:8, KJV). In regards to the record of events occurring on day six of creation, God created animals in the first part of the day and it seems that man was created the latter part of the day.

In Genesis 1:1 it states, "In the beginning God created the heaven and the earth…

> Day 1: God created and divided the light from the darkness.
> Day 2: God created the firmament.
> Day 3: God created dry ground.
> Day 4: God created the sun, moon and stars.
> Day 5: God created fish and birds.
> Day 6: In the morning, God created creatures on the land (He made animals).

> Day 6: In the evening, God created male and female in his own image.

He created the creatures before He created His crowning creation which is man, who was created in His image. So if God created creatures the first half of the day and mankind the latter part of the day, then the animals spent no less than 500 years, as we know it, with God before they were placed under man's dominion. This would suggest that God communicated to the animals and gave them instincts on how to live in a way that would teach survival and bring them under complete submission to a higher calling when necessary. This could be a stretch but my mind will not allow me to rest without wondering how animals are so in tune with the heartbeat of the land and consistently obey the skills and tactics obviously taught before they ever had an encounter with mankind.

During those 500 years they were given instinctive skills regarding how to hunt, when to hunt, and what to hunt for. They have an internal calendar that leads them into mating and migrating seasons. It seems as if they took courses on defending themselves, communication, hibernation, marking their territory, trust, relationship, intimacy, and terrain. All these instincts required to survive were given by God and not man. Tsunami. Earthquakes. Hurricanes. Tornadoes. Wildfires. Landslides. Every type of animal, bird, and creature knows when and where they should go when disasters occur. The beasts and birds of the world were consistent in obeying what they were taught by God.

It wasn't until man came along that blemished the animals. When man became an outcast, because he failed to obey what he had been told by God to NOT do, animals would eventually start to suffer at some point and time. Remember God's crowning creation let Him down, not animals. Man betrayed the call of obedience. The animal kingdom was subjected to mankind prior to the big deception of man. In the 28th and 29th verses we see that God tells male and female that they are to increase in number and rule over the fish of the sea, bird of the air, and over every living creature that moves on the ground. They were told they would be over the creatures of the world but they were not sinful.

In Genesis 2:8 God created Eden, the place where Adam, and later Eve, were placed. God allowed Adam to live in the garden under one condition… that he not eat from the tree of knowledge of good and evil (Gen. 2:17). That's it. Adam was even allowed to name everything on the planet. How cool! Adam had his own place, separate from the others God made and then God created him a helpmate who came from him, just for him. God was happy! He just gave Adam one instruction and it came with a warning... surely you will die. But that didn't stop God's man from being hardheaded.

God was so upset that when He kicked Adam and Eve out of Eden the animals stayed. The only thing that Adam and Eve left with were animal skins for clothes. It's apparent that animals don't think like we do, because they seem to be more in tuned with the earth than we are. That's until man domesticated them. But even then animals are obedient because God put them under man's subjection. So, instead of being able to flee in times of disasters some animals perish because they wait for their master, man, to save them. It's unfortunate that some of us remove the natural instincts of animals because we want a pet. I am a pet lover, an animal lover, so I am the first to be around animals but there are times when I stop to think about how man has removed some animals' dependent connection on God. But for the most part, animals know what to do; it is man who struggles.

THIS SECTION IS FOR MATURE READERS

This section is important because I want you to understand just how important mankind is to God, particularly the children of Israel, who are God's elect. When creating mankind, I believe it was God's climactic moment. It is my belief that He only wanted someone to love Him intimately and unconditionally. Not only did God create male and female, He turned around and created His own special man and gave him his own special woman. God shared His climatic moment with Adam. He even told the male and female to be fruitful and multiple the earth.

It shows that God trusted His creations because the only rules He gave them was to be over the animals and multiply. He specifically told Adam to not eat from the tree of knowledge. He didn't tell everyone else that, just Adam. It shows that when we walk in obedience as Adam did before the fall, it reminds us of God's climactic moment. You make Him feel like He felt when He made mankind and Adam… Good! And obedience makes God feel good, so good, that He declares that moment to be the best He ever felt from eternity past until now (Genesis 1:31). God feels good when His crown and glory is obedient to Him.

Unfortunately, since the fall every human born after that point has been born into a word of sin. Murder, lies, deception, childbirth pains, and so much devastation has been the norm for our lives. I don't believe Eve nor Adam meant to be intentional but it happened because Satan was the only influence they had to refer to at that moment and boy was he a great salesman. As I look around today and watch the news I see that the intimacy that led God to His climactic moment with His creation is now fading and God is not a God who will sit and watch His creation destroy itself.

I believe that God is still so in love with His creation that He gives us the freedom to do as we please as long as we remain obedient to Him. That is a choice that He did not give to the animals or birds. So before you come into true intimacy with God you will experiment with many other temptations of the world with the hopes of validating your existence. You may invest your time and energy into learning about other religions; you may experiment with worldly things such as drugs and other things that may destroy your body; or you may explore your own climatic desires through fornication or adultery. But know this … any act that is contrary to experiencing a true relationship with God is offensive and evil. Basically it is a sin and as I previously stated God does not separate the sin from the sinner. They are both evil things that He despises. Still, the enemy specializes in convincing you that the world and the pleasures of it are not as bad as they seem. He'll whisper to you…

"Everybody is doing it"

"It's okay to try it."

"Don't worry no one else will know!"

"It's your body, so you have a right to do whatever you want to it."

"God will forgive you because He loves the sinner and the sin."

Sounds familiar huh?

Satan will even take what God made to be good and use it against you. Take for instance sex. God rewards us, as procreative creatures, with the feeling of orgasmic pleasure that sex brings. While sex was intended to be used behind the sacred doors of holy matrimony, between a male and a female, it has become the place many people journey to for intense enjoyment and release exclusively. And while this feeling was designed with a purpose we have been guilty of using sex as an act to fulfill the need to be wanted by another. Women, and some men, use their bodies as a way to earn a living or to feel wanted by both male and female instead of finding the true love of God. Eventually, sex becomes an addiction.

Be honest, unless you have committed to a life of celibacy then you have been sexually tempted. In some point in your life, you have had a sexual encounter with someone with whom you were not contractually bound to, also known as you were not married to. We have all had moments where we had sex out of marriage. Some of you may not be married now but you still have what the world considers "desires." Let me be clear, having sex out of wedlock is called fornication and adultery, if you are married and it is a sin that God is not pleased with and you will be judged (1 Corinthians 6:9-20). But that's how disobedience does us. We believe we need sexual satisfaction when we really need to focus on being obedient to God. As we seek the acceptance and pleasure of being wanted and desired, God has the same desire with us.

While we have difficulty describing exactly how a sexual climax feels, God describes His most intimate experience when man was created as good! Some may believe and even agree that a particular sexual escapade is the greatest feeling in the body. I tend to believe that nothing feels better to the body, mind, and soul than walking in obedience unto God. You cannot be in agreement with me if you've never had the encounter of living an obedient life. Walking in obedience was intended to be a feeling that lasts eternally, not 30-45 seconds. Obedience to God, while a lifelong journey, is still a journey that brings eternal satisfaction to all parts of you. It also brings a peace to you unlike no other peace. That's why the serpent tempted Eve in the Garden because he knew she was the weaker of the two. The serpent didn't want God to have that satisfaction any longer that he had with Adam. The serpent (Satan) is still at it to this day.

Satan is upset with God because before man had the crown he wore it. He was the apple of God's affection and when God saw that Satan was out to be Him, and that he wanted the kingdom of heaven, he was kicked out of heaven. Satan was so devious that he took a third of the heavenly host with him when he was banished from Heaven. In his descent to earth, where he rules, he pledged that he will destroy all that God loves. And what God loves without a shadow of a doubt is man. Satan even goes about the earth looking to destroy what God created as it shows in Job 2:2. That's why it is important for us to stand bold on being obedient to God.

Here is where the message of obedience comes home. Walking in obedience to God is your way of making Him feel good and with that feeling comes benefits. You have access to everything you can see and touch in the Garden and in the Promised Land. Adam and Eve had a problem with obedience; they wanted what they were commanded not to have. Could it have been innocent curiosity? Perhaps. But curiosity killed the cat and it led to blatant disobedience to a direct command from God. Although we are called God's crowning creation we will always be beautifully imperfect creatures who were placed in an imperfect world. We will struggle with unbelief and disobeying the very mandates of God. I promise you it will happen! But, the lessons learned from our forefathers will prove our faith as we continue to walk through the wilderness and gain wisdom from those who make wisdom their Master.

God was well aware of the Serpent's presence in the Garden. God was prepared for the pouncing of Eve and subsequently Adam. But having all wisdom, God also knew that an innocent man would not bring Him as much glory as a redeemed man would. Yes, sin is the problem that leads to disobeying God but the problem has been rectified following and obeying God. God even gave us a special gift to show that He still desires to see us in obedience with Him. That means He has not given up on us yet. That's the good news! That grace still abounds and it can become our ultimate comeback story.

CHAPTER | TWO

OBEDIENCE HAS POWER

Philip and Melissa were the most admired couple in the college ministry group at their church. The way they would share brief glances at each other during worship service was a great witness of their heated love. They'd only been married a little over a year when the church decided to surprise them with a late honeymoon gift. The gift included a two-night stay at a log cabin that belonged to one of the seasoned members of the church. The couple didn't get to have a "real" honeymoon after the wedding because it was discovered shortly after the wedding through a routine checkup that Melissa was pregnant with twins.

This getaway would be something special because it had been months since they were able to take off and just enjoy one another. They welcomed the gift and set off for the cabin. When they arrived, the cold winter night caused them to cozy up by the fireplace. Philip eyed a nice brick pit that would be perfect in helping cap off the night as he prepared a nice dinner for his bride. After a relaxing couple of hours by the fire Phillip took a log off the fire with the tongs and placed it under the screen of the grill to lock in that smoke flavor they both loved to taste in their food.

"This is going to be a fantastic evening" he thought to himself.

After dinner ended and the fire went out they turned in for the night. Unfortunately, they were awoken from their sleep to the sound of a siren and a great commotion in the back. There was a small fire that had quickly rose and was moving towards the main road where other cabins were located. After the fire department sifted through the small grass fire they discovered that a small piece of the firewood had been blown off the grill onto the ground. A moment of carelessness on the part of the cook almost resulted in a weekend of regret because of misplaced fire. The same fire in the wood used to keep them cozy could have been the cause of a major catastrophe!

Misplaced fire can be a problem if not handled appropriately. Obedience is the fire power needed to ignite your faith and lead you to living abundantly. As Jesus walked in obedience, the fire of God in His life was always used obediently. This power was not used to destroy, but rather to produce. Outside of Job, Jesus was the only man who lived a life of total obedience. His walk, though hard, was a perfect walk because He made sure that He harkened to the word of God. Basically Jesus walked in obedience, which pleased God. The power Jesus used when He walked this earth was willingly given to Him as long as He obeyed the will of His Father.

Let me take a moment to break down the word power. By definition power is defined as "energy that can do work." But what does that mean? Can something have power without work? When you think about it, much of the energy around us seems pretty powerful but unless it is actually accomplishing something it is not really delivering power. For example, some experts say that a lightning strike releases 15 million volts of electricity. That is a lot of energy! But since we are unable to harness this energy to help us light our homes, operate machinery, and do other tasks that require electricity, lightening really produces no power.

The same principle holds true in the spiritual realm. The scriptures tell us that Jesus baptizes us with the Holy Spirit and fire (Matthew 3:11). When the Lord pours out the fire of His presence, it can either release great power to set us free and overcome the enemy or it can produce wild fires in us which, though they may seem spectacular, can result in great damage. The damage is caused when we are all over the place in the Word of God. We fail to use God's fire to be set free and to set others free, instead we wield the Word of God like a sword to destroy other believers. You know the person who does all the condemnation of others but never see their own sin? But when we use it to set free and become free then we are using God's power and His fiery presence to stay in line and be obedient.

The power of obedience has always been an assurance to the children of the Most High. From Genesis to Revelation, the Bible has a lot to say about obedience. The powerful result of obedience was seen when the three Hebrew men who were thrown in the furnace when they refused to bow their knees to the golden image. God himself protected them and destroyed their enemies (Daniel 3:8-30). God's power was seen in the protection of Daniel who would rather face a den of hungry lions than to stop praying to a living Lord (Daniel 6:16-24). The obedience of Israel applying the Passover blood to their houses released the power of God on their behalf and brought them out of Egyptian bondage. In each of these cases, we see that when we do our part, which always involves obedience, then God's supercharged blessings often seem ridiculous to the natural minds of men.

Obedience is the true test of your love for God and the secret to discovering God's will for your life. If you ever wondered what God's will is for your life you would be wise to follow His commandments. Yes, keeping His commandments is what God considers obedience. No, the commandments were NOT done away with when Christ came. That's a common misconception and many are lost because they believe they no longer have to keep the Most High's commandments. It's in His commandments that we discover His will for our lives and His unconditional love. Jesus clearly states that in Matthew 19:16-18.

When we focus on everything except being obedient, we begin to struggle with questions about our future. Questions like: How can I know God's plan for my life? Which job should I take? Is this the person God wants me to marry? Is this a good investment to make? Should I share the gospel with my boss? You probably have questions you could add to that list. But the one thing I know about these questions is that I always asked them when I was living in disobedience. It was as if I never had an answer and my life was always in turmoil. But the greatest discovery I ever made concerning how to know the will of God involves the following:

- Fully surrendering my life to the Lordship of Christ
- Living a life of obedience through the power of the Holy Spirit
- Maintaining my first love to the Lord

Many Christians are trying so hard to discover the will of God that they lose the joy of the Lord and the love they once had for Him fades away. They focus so much on being a "Super Christian" that they remove the joy of living in obedience. I can guess it's because living an obedient life seems like there is little to no joy, but that is so far from the truth. It is my belief that all we need to do is maintain our first love for Him, walk in the power of the Holy Spirit, and we will be in the very will of God. So as you continue to walk in the Spirit, He will guide you in making the most important decisions of your life. He will also guide you in the daily, moment-by-moment decisions and actions of your life.

Speaking of the Holy Spirit, Jesus says, *"When He, the Spirit of truth, comes, He will guide you into all truth...and He will tell you what is yet to come."* (John 16:13, KJV) So the key to knowing God's will is to be obedient to the guidance of the Holy Spirit of truth. If you are willing to trust and obey God and live a holy life, then God will reveal

Himself to you and direct your steps as a way of life. Satan, on the other hand, is the enemy of our soul. His mission is to keep you from being effective and fruitful in your witnessing. Although he yields great power, Satan can never defeat you if you are completely yielded and obedient to Christ. We have to be willing to stand in obedience in order to defeat every attack of Satan. It is challenging, especially when you have people around you who live in contented disobedience. But we have to fight through it.

Unfortunately, some people are reluctant to trust God completely with their lives, fearing that He may want to make a change in the plans they already have for their lives. Yes, God will change your plans. His plans are infinitely better than the very best you can ever conceive. I think that is where we get out of alignment with God. We make our own plans and expect to follow them, versus us following the plan that He has for our lives. I once lived that life. I would write down what I wanted to do and needed to do to go to the next level but I quickly learned, as I shared in my first book, *The Trial of My Faith*, that my plans are rarely ever the plans of God, especially if we are out of alignment and living in disobedience. I learned then that obedience brings with it uncertainties that challenge our will and shatter those feelings of comfort that we cherish so much. Although obedience brings ultimate freedom it does not bring instant joy.

Obedience has nothing to do with feelings. Unfortunately, for so many believers, their spiritual walk is not made up of obedience to God, but obedience to their feelings. Their theme song should be, "feelings...nothing more than feelings," but "right feeling is produced by obedience, never vice versa," as Oswald Chambers states. Obedience brings right feelings, not the other way around. We don't only obey that which we feel like obeying, nor do we only obey when we feel like it.

Ask yourself this ... how could an army function if its soldiers only obeyed orders when they felt like obeying? Just imagine a soldier saying, "I obeyed your orders, Sir. I went to the front lines, but I felt like delivering pizza rather than ammo." Can't relate? Then would you want a spouse who only upholds the marriage covenant when he/she feels like it? Can you hear them uttering these words to you, "It wasn't adultery, I just felt single today!"

Are you following me? Obedience is an action, not a reaction. It is an exercise of our wills. It is a decision that needs to be practiced. If disobedience brings catastrophic consequences, then the wisdom to live obediently has monumental advantages. The creatures that make an appearance in this book will teach us through their behavior how to achieve daily success and survive insurmountable odds by simply obeying their God-given instincts. Wildlife seems to have a will that, at times, overlooks justifiable logic but trust me they are instinctively following that which was placed in them by God to do what He created them to do and when He created them to do it.

To obey instincts, or greater wisdom, to the point of death is something that can be learned but not necessarily taught. Our experiences with God, in life, are lessons to be cherished and shared with even the casual Christian or obstinate observer. An ant, for instance, is a tiny thing, a mere speck crawling upon the ground. Most people might think there is little they can learn from such a seemingly insignificant creature. However, in some ancient cultures, ants were venerated as productive and wise insects. Their teamwork and perseverance enable them to build grand cities (mounds). This proves how new lessons can be gleaned from unlikely creatures such as ants, chimpanzees, horses, elephants, and dolphins.

Some of the blessings the Lord intends for us to enjoy come only by believing and obeying Him against impossible odds. He would even have us to learn obedience via examples provided through the natural instincts of animals. God delights in obedience because His commandments are not too hard. This is good news! Deuteronomy 30:11 says, *"This commandment which I command you this day is not too hard for you."* And 1 John 5:3 says, *"This is the love of God, that we keep His commandments. And His commandments are not burdensome."* His commandments are only as hard to obey as would be His glory to cherish or His promises to believe. When God selected the Israelites to be His special people, it seemed to be on an "if-then" basis. If they obeyed, then He would always bless. If they disobeyed, then they would be cursed. Unfortunately, they experienced more curses than blessings because most of them failed to learn the wisdom that led to obedience. But despite their constant disobedience, God remained faithful to Israel because they were His chosen people. He did allow them into captivity several times and to experience hardships over the years and to this day, but His love for Israel still gleams bright.

Here are three reasons for obedience to God:

1. A duty to be performed.
2. A debt to be paid.
3. A delight to be preferred.

Obedience is a duty to be performed because this was the modeled requirement which God introduced when He covered Adam and Eve with the first animal slain to cover their sin. While there is no documentation to prove this, it is obvious that Adam and Eve were taught how to offer sacrifices as a way to repent to God. We observe this when we learned that Abel's offering was acceptable, but Cain's was not. It is obvious by their offerings that they were taught this duty by their parents. Obedience is a debt to be paid because there was an offense that needed to be repented for. In the court of God's righteous law, sin could not be looked upon. So, there has to be a way to payback God in order to get back to the right relationship that has been lost. This would serve as a temporary covering until Jesus the Christ paid the ultimate price at Calvary.

Here's a question. Does God smell?

Apparently He does and He finds pleasure in it. In the Bible, God mentions His pleasure with aroma 39 times and on 16 different occasions in the book of Leviticus alone. So, since God does have the sense of smell, what things smell good to Him?

Obedience is a delight to be preferred because the scent of obedience served as a pivotal requirement during Israel's journey through the wilderness and beyond. For God, obedience has a scent and the sense of smell is a rather amazing gift God has given us. God used sacrifice as a way to please His senses. That sacrifice gave Israel the opportunity to please God's senses. Imagine where we might be without the fragrance of obedience? If God rejected the sacrifice of our forefathers, then we would be lost. Just like we enjoy the fragrance from a lilac tree, freshly mowed lawns or hay fields, a freshly peeled piece of fruit, God enjoys the fragrance of our obedience.

Obedience smells good to God and it has its own aroma to Him. In fact the smell of the lamb and goat being sacrificed in Samuel reminded King Saul that being obedient is better than to sacrifice (1 Samuel 15:22). Years later David wrote in Psalms 51:16-17, "*you do not delight in sacrifice or I would bring it you do not take pleasure in burnt offerings the sacrifices of God are a broken spirit a broken and contrite heart oh God you will not despise.*"

So, obedience has its own type of smell and this was God's favorite smell in the Old Testament. Specifically, the aroma of a sacrifice is important to God. The importance of a sacrifice's aroma is not the smell but what the smell represents - the substitutionary atonement for sin. The very first mention of God smelling the aroma of a burnt offering is found in Genesis 8:21. Noah offered a burnt offering of clean animals and birds after leaving the ark. We are told that it was a "pleasing" aroma to God. The idea is that Noah's sacrifice was a propitiation, or satisfaction, of God's righteous requirement. God was pleased with the sacrifice and then gave the promise to never again destroy every living creature with a flood.

In Leviticus, a pleasing aroma is mentioned in connection with the various offerings in the tabernacle worships of the Jews. Leviticus 1:9 says, "*The priest is to burn all of it on the altar. It is a burnt offering, a food offering, an aroma pleasing to the LORD.*" As in the case of Noah's offering, what pleased the Lord was the commitment to offer worship in His name as He commanded. The "pleasing aroma" is also mentioned in Leviticus 1:9 and 13, emphasizing the action of propitiation rather than the actual smoke of the burnt offering.

The same is true in Leviticus 2 regarding the grain offering. Despite the fact that this offering involved grain rather than meat, it had *"an aroma pleasing to the LORD"* (verse 2). Even the larger sacrifice at the yearly Feast of Weeks focused on the redemption of sinners as the reason for the pleasing aroma. Leviticus 23:18 states, *"Present with this bread seven male lambs, each a year old and without defect, one young bull and two rams. They will be a burnt offering to the LORD, together with their grain offerings and drink offerings - a food offering, an aroma pleasing to the LORD."*

The New Testament reveals Christ as the final sacrifice for sin, the ultimate propitiation in Ephesians 5:2, *"Christ loved us and gave himself up for us as a fragrant offering and sacrifice to God."* Jesus, the Son of God, was the only One who could provide the eternally pleasing sacrifice. He alone is the One of whom the Father says, "You are my Son, whom I love; with you I am well pleased." A life lived in obedience is a life that gives an aroma that is accepted and attracts the nostrils of God. This is amazing and concerning as well. If obedience is the smell He desires, then the opposite would create a stench. I dare not think of the many times we have turned the nostrils of our Heavenly Father by allowing the stench of our lives to approach His holy presence. Our daily lives, if possible, must make God sick to His stomach. We live lives according to the world instead of the Word in the Bible and I am sure that is not a life of obedience. Therefore, we must remember that any sacrifice that is promoted by obedience is a pleasing aroma to God.

It's time to bring a smile back to God's face as He inhales a sweet aroma from our life instead of a stench that turns His head and breaks His heart. Dietrich Bonhoeffer is quoted as saying, "One act of obedience is better than one hundred sermons." In Romans 5:19, *"For just as through the disobedience of the one man the many were made sinners, so also through the obedience of the one man the many will be made righteous."* We must get back to fearing doing anything counter to living in obedience. We must get back to being a pleasant aroma to God by living an obedient life.

CHAPTER | THREE

FEARFULLY WONDERFULLY

If anyone asks you what you learned reading this chapter, tell them "you are 98.5 percent chimp, 97 percent orangutan, and 75 percent worm."

An article I read on Yahoo! News caught my eye. The title read, Are we humans or animals or both? According to scientists, orangutans share 97 percent of their DNA with humans! They are more closely related to us than previously thought. Chimpanzees share 98.5 percent of their DNA with humans. Chimpanzees use coconut shells as a cup to drink water, they crack nuts with small logs or rocks, and they can walk upright. If tickled, chimpanzees giggle! But unlike humans, they have the ability to giggle while exhaling and inhaling.

Try it out!

But seriously, are we 98.5 percent chimp and just 1.5 percent human? Interestingly enough, scientists conducted a study on a soil-dwelling worm called a nematode. Scientists found that the nematode shares 75 percent of its DNA with humans. What does that mean? Does it mean that when God made us He looked at Chimpanzees, Orangutans, or worms as a blueprint when He was making His man? Does it mean that we have been wrong about being made in God's image? Science would definitely make you think twice about where you came from.

But here is what Genesis 1:25 tells us about animals, "God made the wild animals according to their kinds, the livestock according to their kinds, and all the creatures that move along the ground according to their kinds. And God saw that it was good." Genesis 1:26-28 (NIV) tells us how God created man. "Then God said, 'Let us make man in our image, in our likeness, and let them rule over the fish of the sea and the birds of the air, over the livestock, over all the earth, and over all the creatures that move along the ground.' So God created man in His own image, in the image of God He created Him male and female He created them. God blessed them and said to them, 'Be fruitful and increase in number; fill the earth and subdue it. Rule over the fish of the sea and the birds of the air and over every living creature that moves on the ground.'"

Look at what God says in Genesis 1:31 (NIV) after He creates man, "God saw all that He had made, and it was very good. And there was evening, and there was morning— the sixth day." So that means that man is unique among everything created by God because God created man in His own image. According to God's word, we are unique among everything created. So after God creates animals, He declares everything to be, "good." But after He creates man, He declares everything to be, "very good."

Why the difference? Why is the creation of chimps and orangutans good, while the creation of man is very good?

Our answer is repeatedly emphasized, four times, in Genesis 1:26-27. Unlike animals, we've been endowed with a capacity to reflect the image of our creator! We reflect His very likeness, His character, His attributes, His righteousness, and His holiness. This is what makes human life so special, so unique, and so sacred! We are the only creatures in all of creation capable of reflecting God's holy character and glory. Not animals, regardless of their ability to drink from coconut cups or giggle when tickled.

The human tragedy is that we identify more with chimps than with God, who created us to be holy. So here is the thing about chimpanzees and about animals in general. They live in the flesh, in the moment. They are hard-wired to follow their desires and thoughts, their fleshly cravings and their natural instincts. Chimpanzees do not transcend their animal nature. They descend into it. But here is what is unique about human beings. God endows us with a spiritual capacity to transcend the flesh. You are uniquely special in the eyes of God. You should tell yourself this in those times when you feel like you're being crushed on every side with the problems this present world may bring.

You are special to God. You were created as God's workmanship and to do good works that trillions of animal and creatures cannot. God loves you and He chose you to do His will. Animals were created for nutrition and in some cases companionship. The very thought of you makes God's heart skip a beat. You are an exceptional individual. You are so precious in God's eyes that He put His "personal touch" on you. He gave you life by sharing His own breath. This sets you apart from any other creature including angels. Have you ever stopped to think about what that really means?

The Hebrew root of the Latin phrase for image of God is imago Dei which means image, shadow or likeness of God. At the very least this means humans occupy a higher place in the created order because we alone are imprinted with godlike characteristics. That means that you have been fearfully and wonderfully made (Psalm 139:14).

Do you ever wake up, take a good look in the mirror, and tell yourself, "No doubt about it I'm fearfully and wonderfully made!" Maybe when you think about the kind of person you are and words like "average" or "not bad" come to mind. But if you ever consider yourself unremarkable or even ordinary, then you're not seeing yourself as a result of God's divine creation. When we discover the truth that we are God's unique design, it becomes overwhelming because God honored us by fearfully and wonderfully making the Word flesh (John 1:1, 14), clothing the Son of God with a body like ours; then clothing our fleshly body with a glory like His.

On a more practical level, God has fearfully and wonderfully made us, setting us apart as the brightest, clearest mirror of God's creativity. While evolutionary biology considers us nothing more than glorified apes, scientific research confirms that humans are vastly unique on many levels. We often mistakenly equate this with just physical appearance. God transcends all that is physical and spatial. It is the very soul of human beings that especially bears God's image: mind, will, and emotion. God's image on us consists of knowledge, righteousness, and true holiness (Ephesians 4:24; Colossians 3:10). Man's capacity for abstract thinking and unconditional love sets us apart from animals. Humans are unique in that we recognize wrongdoing and seek redemption.

American author and biochemist, Isaac Asimov (1919–1992), stated that the human brain is "... the most complex and orderly arrangement of matter in the universe." As you read this, your brain signals your eyes to automatically adjust the focus and aperture. Humans are not the product of chance or haphazard construction. We are NOT the descendants of monkeys, apes or other wildlife. We are NOT some jungle science experiments who evolved. We ARE the chosen creation of God. Mankind is His creation but the Israelites are His particular people.

Let me break it down a little bit more. In the time it took you to read any of the previous paragraphs, 1.5 gallons (6 liters) of blood passed through your heart. Did you know that the human heart's blood vessels are not just straight through tubes? They are helical, having a slight twist to them. This gentle corkscrewing makes your blood flow more evenly, minimizing damage from turbulent flow, especially at T-junctions. This smooth flow also encourages the productions of health by promoting protective substances. God's attention to the human heart is extraordinary. In many cultures, the heart is seen as the center of the emotions. The human heart is fearfully and wonderfully made, enabling us to love and experience God intimately. The heart reveals our personality, thoughts, memories, emotions, desires, and will (Luke 6:45). Our hearts not only think, feel, and remember, but also choose every course of action. Still our decisions should reflect integrity of heart, with a heart that is discerning. When we live an upright and honorable life, God fills our hearts with joy (Psalm 97:11). God also places a high value on our bodies as well as our hearts. We are an intricate and fleshly fine tuning of divine wisdom, a creation "a little lower than heavenly beings" but capable of being the crown of honor and glory (Psalm 8:5).

So, the next time you look in the mirror, see yourself as God does, "fearfully and wonderfully made," designed to "Love the Lord your God with all your heart and with all your soul and with all your mind," (Matthew 22:37) because you were made in the image of God. Some believe that saying that you are made in God's image is an audacious claim and one that carries a tremendous amount of responsibility. But, if the unbeliever should ever want to get a glimpse of the Lord, they should be able to see Him in you. Your godliness is the path to your greatest fulfillment and once you understand who you are this image can be maintained. You will feel the greatest pleasure and wholeness when the person God made you to be is fully developed and expressed.

CHAPTER | FOUR

TRAINING DAY: THE WISDOM THAT HUNGERS

"…there we sat around pots of meat and ate all the food we wanted, but you have brought us out into this desert to starve this entire assembly to death."
- Exodus 16:3 NIV

As far back as I can remember our family always had a dog. I have never gone more than two years without man's best friend at my side. My wife, Mary, is not a lover of dogs as I am. After we were married, I always knew the subject of owning a dog would have to happen soon. So when the time was right I said, "I think we need a dog," but the breed of dog was not agreed upon.

To my chagrin, Mary stated, "If we're going to get one it must be a house dog." She suggested something small, like a Maltese or a Yorkshire Terrier.

My response, "Never," because I wanted a Rottweiler.

You see, I am similar to Peter the disciple, not the apostle. I tend to have a strong will and a loud personality. I have often been labeled as stubborn. So, more time lapsed. More persuasion occurred. We made the final decision to get a dog. Our neighbors, just around the corner, bred German Rottweilers. I imagined early morning jogs and walks with my dog, intimidating what I thought to be lesser breeds along our paths. I was convinced any evildoers would be reluctant to approach a home where he heard a deep growl accompanied with a stealth physique and aggressive behaviors. Intimidation would be our first line of defense. I was excited. However, before I could get my dog, I'd have to install a run fence and invest in obedience training for the dog. A dog of that size and disposition requires boundaries and constant reminders of who was in charge.

So $1,800 and seven months later, we welcomed "Selah" to her new home. Brian, our dog trainer, kept her at his house for the first three months to bring her under submission in a new environment. He would teach her how to obey in ways that I could not. Once training was complete and all vaccinations were current, it was time for her to come home permanently. Her understanding and obedience was phenomenal. She could "sit", "stay", "chase the ball", and other commands, better than any other dog I'd ever owned. I asked Brian what was the key to getting her to obey so soon?

He said, "The key to her obedience was the growl in her stomach. Never feed her too much." He suggested one small cup in the morning and one cup or a few treats at night. "The growl in her stomach," he expressed to us, "would always remind her of her training."

What Brian did, as a part of the training, was to give her a treat only after she obeyed a command. When she didn't obey, she did not get fed. He further added that a dog that is always full is a dog too satisfied to obey and would probably lie around and do nothing that complimented her training. According to Brian, a stuffed dog is a sluggish dog. Her obedience training was conducted before the sun rose, before her morning meal. Now that she lives with me, this slight hunger in her stomach is still a constant reminder of her early morning training. Keeping her stomach under submission is the key to her obedience.

Although it can be known as a continent of contradictions, food is always on the mind. Hunger is that gnawing ache on the inside of you; that sense of need that is not content until it is filled. Hunger is an active state, for it results in you seeking out the object of desire that will satisfy your need. God used hunger to train His children. Some of the most pivotal moments during the children of Israel's development occurred when their stomachs were growling. These episodes reveal to those of us who have studied their history that they, too, were in need of obedience training. Although they left Egypt after eating the Passover supper the night before (Exodus 12:1-8), and taking with them great flocks and herds (Exodus 12:32), 75 days later they appeared to be starving. During this time of hunger, the children of Israel rose against Moses, revealing their true character. They were not truly starving, but rather grumbling. Nehemiah 9:21 tells us that when the Israelites wandered for 40 years they lacked nothing. This means they didn't lack food. When they grumbled they weren't starving, they merely didn't want what the Lord had provided because they wanted something else, perhaps delicacies and portions they once had in Egypt. Recall in Exodus 16:3 the Israelites' claim of starving was accompanied by the lament, *"when we sat by the pots of meat and when we ate bread to the full!"*

They hungered for what they missed but were not starving and this is when God begins to train them how to have a hunger for the things of God. The nation of Israel had a problem obeying the commands of God through Moses. They didn't come when He called. They dragged along when they were supposed to be walking in obedience. They made a mess of everything good that He gave them. They talked too loud, talked too much, or didn't care to talk to Him at all. They wanted everything except what He gave them.

On several occasions they attacked the leadership of Moses and bit the hand that was appointed to feed them.

"We want meat," they cried. "We want bread!" they shouted. "We want to be satisfied." But what Israel failed to learn was that feeding only comes after obedience. As our quest to feed the physical man happens several times throughout the day, the spiritual man needs sustenance to survive as well. What you feed the growl is what fuels the faith. This kind of hunger can only be satisfied by walking in obedience to God. Walking the journey of faith can only be successful when there are acts of obedience that follow. There is an order to be carried in faith. God never places an order on your life that He's not prepared to fill. Obedience is the fruit of faith and when you produce fruit your hunger dissipates and you become satisfied with your relationship with God. If you are one who struggles with solving the problem of disobedience in your life, then the wisdom to resolve it is found in feeding the growl with something from God's menu.

The way you determine if there is sin (disobedience) in your life while you are seeking more of God is by the amount of hunger pains you have that never seem to be satisfied. This deep growl is a void that only God can feed. Unfortunately, we try to feed it with worldly food but the result is disobedience to the will of God. So, in order to bring Israel under the arm of obedience, the Lord allowed them to get hungry. It was an opportunity to learn how to find satisfaction in what God offered and not what they believed they needed.

In the animal kingdom, a world in which things are done differently, there is a common theme. Every creature needs to eat in order to live and as prophetic people we need to hunger and thirst after God. Those who have a hunger for God need to be just as aggressive as a predator is in order to catch its next meal. If there is no aggressive chase, the growl will continue until fed, lest the animal dies. While animals have been subjected to the order of the wild kingdom, humans are the toughest species to bring under submission.

Humans are more concerned with having than being and we choose dominance over dependence. Therefore, God takes us through the wilderness to bring us back in the order and authority we were given in the Garden of Eden. God put Israel in a place that would teach them to hear His voice, train them how to live, and to learn their true identity as His chosen people. Today, God wants us to catch the wisdom that leaves us to totally depend on Him. God won't make you obey, but He can make the conditions so uncomfortable that you will either submit to Him or die in disobedience. When we run from God and hide in our disobedience we live a life of discontentment and hardships. What we should do is naturally run to His loving embrace so that we are protected from the harness of the world. Instead we are the only species who run faster in the wrong direction, which is away from God and the obedience of His will.

You must have a hunger for God before you can hear from God. John Piper says in his book, *A Hunger for God*, "If you don't feel strong desires for the manifestation of the glory of God, it is not because you have drunk deeply and are satisfied. It is because you have nibbled so long at the table of the world. Your soul is stuffed with small things, and there is no room for the great."

That is a shouting moment!

We consume so much of the world that when it's time to hear from God we are too full and think we can survive in the world alone. We don't realize that it's the other way around; we need the WORD of God instead the WORLD. Do you understand what I am saying? You fill up on acknowledgements, titles and other things that the world offers that you lose your ability and desire to hunger for what God has for you. That's why we have to starve (fast) ourselves from the world so we can have an endless hunger for God.

Fasting

My suggestion for anyone desiring God is to fast and pray. "Christian fasting, at its root, is the hunger of homesickness for God. A hunger for God," says John Piper. When Jesus began His ministry, He was led into the wilderness to fast for 40 days. He had no contact with human beings. Jesus was alone in the wilderness except for the presence of Satan who tormented Him while angels strengthened Him to endure. When fasting, you'll discover how powerful you are and how powerless Satan is. Satan cannot combat the power given during your time of fasting and seeking God. He is defenseless if you make a statement that you are seeking to get closer to the Most High.

Fasting must be done in an attitude of humility (Deuteronomy 8:3). It is not necessary for others to know you are fasting because it is directed towards God. *"But when you fast, put oil on your head and was your face, so that it will not be obvious to men that you are fasting, but only to your Father, who is unseen; and your Father, who sees what is done in secret, will reward you,"* (Matthew 6:17-18). Biblical fasting brings us to a closer union with God. While our bodies are being deprived of food and water for the purpose of drawing near to God, He has promised in return to draw near to us. This is a spiritual certainty. As we decrease, the Spirit increases. We are strengthened and renewed. "*...Though outwardly we are wasting away, yet inwardly we are being renewed day by day,"* (2 Corinthians 4:16). There's a growl on the inside. Don't ignore it, but fill it with the things that please God. One bite from His table and you will never know hunger again. Oh taste and see that the Lord is good (Psalm 34:8).

One final thing about fasting... the true meaning of fasting is to completely cut off eating and drinking. Modern fasting tells us that we can eat a little or drink a little but when we fast we must submit our bodies and spirit to God so that we are able to hear from God. I am not telling you to not eat or drink, especially if you have medical concerns, but what I am telling you is that you must follow the guidelines of God. Fasting allows you to open yourself up to God and trust Him with everything, even your body. But please consult with your doctor, especially if you have health concerns regarding biblical fasting.

CHAPTER | FIVE

AND WISDOM KEEPS CALLING

"Does not wisdom call out? Does not understanding raise her voice? At the highest point along the way, where the paths meet, she takes her stand."
- Proverbs 8:1-2

The Wisdom That Runs Wild

There are times in our lives when we get to certain places and all of a sudden we are at a standstill. We are driving solo. We try to radio God but it seems as though He does not hear us at all. Has there ever been a time in your life when you have been alone? Has there ever been a time in your life when you had no one to turn to, no place to go? You look for words of encouragement, words of comfort and direction, but to no avail. You call your best friend. They are not answering the phone. You call your mother, but she is not home. Your father is out on business or just out of your life. Your girlfriend is oblivious to the real you and your boyfriend has no time to talk. If you have been in these places, if you've had such an experience, then you have been in the wilderness.

But what is this wilderness?

Wilderness, eremia in Aramaic, is an uninhabited place. There is nothing there, nobody is there. There is no vegetation, no water to quench your thirst. It is like being a traveler in a vast desert. The wilderness is like being lost in that place out West, called Death Valley. The wilderness goes beyond a physical place. Your wilderness may not be a desert. It may be in being single. Your wilderness may be in financial difficulties. Your wilderness may be bad business decisions. Your wilderness may be a child who won't do right. The wilderness is that time in life when everything is one color. However, the wilderness can be a blessing. God wants us alone, sometimes; He puts us in the wilderness to cut away the junk. The wilderness can be a hot desert that God uses to burn away the grotesque that is our sins.

The wilderness is a time when you are alone, wandering, wondering, asking the question - Where am I? Who am I? What am I supposed to be doing with my life? You feel that no one can do anything for you. You've prayed, rebuked devils, and fasted, yet you still find yourself in a barren place. But do not despair unto death. The wilderness comes right before the fulfillment of the promise God makes to all of His children. Even Jesus wandered in the wilderness until it was time for Him to receive the promise that God instructed Him to give to the lost children of Israel, and to the Northern tribes of Israel that God put away because they refused to not worship false idols. Jesus was only sent for restoration of Israel (Matthew 5:14) and when He was sent He experienced time in the wilderness to prepare Himself to become the sacrifice for Israel.

Here is a revelation for you who hear me … God uses us and we must go through the wilderness to get to the other side where there is milk and honey. It is unavoidable. God wants to know He can trust you. He already knows what we will do so He puts us to the test. He wants us to rise to the ethical challenge of the wilderness. You may not be a lover of animals as I am, but if you study the behavior and the complete surrender that animals give to their owners, you will notice they surrender to the God given instincts that was put in them from their creation in the beginning. Knowing this you might be tempted enough to change from the casual animal gazer into a student of their acuity. We can learn from the animals that without pause are extremely obedient to the inner growl that was given to them by God. With proper attention paid to the internal growl of animals you will be able to apply their obedience to the survival in your life and learn how to live abundantly. No. I am not telling you to act like an animal. I am simply letting you know that you can and will learn a lot about obedience through animals.

Our world is home to over 5 million different kinds of species. With more than 5 million different species come more than 5 million different ways of living, 5 million different ways of responding to danger and 5 million different ways of surviving. However, we all share in a few commonalities that prove to be vital to every species. We have to eat in order to live. We have to struggle in order to survive. We all have to grow in order to continue the life cycle. But one of the hardest lessons for human beings to learn is to obey God instantly and instinctively. The wilderness is where there is an amazing opportunity to witness the wild animals' way of survival that cannot be seen in the city lights. I believe there is wisdom learned from wildlife that should aide us in our obedience to God. What better place to take a rebellious nation than to a hot bed of survival seen on a daily basis?

I don't want you to see this wilderness as a wilderness per se. For those reading who have spiritual awareness, you can see it as an incubator that will lead Israel back to the level of intimacy they once had and what God wants. When disobedience entered in the Garden, it was dealt with by God's wisdom. When disobedience entered after the journey out of bondage, the wilderness became a place where God brought

Israel under submission by allowing some to make their arrival to the Promise Land and some to perish during the 40 years. When God freed the Israelites from Egypt into the wilderness, it was not a wilderness at all; it was much more than that. It was an incubator, but you'll need to look at it through your spiritual eyes.

An incubator facilitates various forms of incubation. It is used to grow and maintain microbiological or cell cultures. Incubators provide care for premature babies in a neonatal intensive-care unit. Often, babies who are born prematurely will be placed in an incubator until they have become strong enough to be housed in a regular crib. The incubator serves as the babies' first lesson of intimacy outside the mother's womb. Up until the time of birth, a baby knows nothing but the mother. They are physically connected to each other by the umbilical cord. They will never experience this type of intimacy again, not even in breast feeding. It is a feeling of closeness and when the mother's heart beats the baby feels it. When the baby is uncomfortable the mother is uncomfortable. When the baby is hungry, the mother is hungry. However, when the baby is born, the world of comfort he or she once knew is gone. Now the baby has to fight on its own and if it is premature, the incubator is put in place to aide in the struggle. There is a connection that cannot be compared or completely explained unless you've been pregnant. And, while everyone cannot be a witness to being pregnant with child, we all are pregnant with purpose. God places Israel into an incubator so they can be close to him. He wanted the intimacy He lost in the Garden.

The incubator, wilderness, is where Israel realizes that God is responsible for all that they see and all that they would become. That is the purpose of life when you live serving God. Life is a setup and it has been so since the onset of the creation of man. Life is an invitation to respond to the overtures of a God who loves us and desires to share His life with us.

Think about it.

God birthed a nation who reminded Him of His children, Adam and Eve and just as He casted Adam and Eve out, He casted Israel out into the wilderness because they inherited the problem of disobedience from their parents. God used the wilderness to nurture and develop Israel in its premature state. Though Israel desired meat, God gave them milk. Let's look at that another way. Israel was not ready for meat (the word of God) so He gave them milk. Milk represented the wisdom infancy of Israel, despite them being a mighty nation once before. But, it was their forefathers' disobedience that took them into captivity in Egypt and it was their disobedience when they left Egypt that sent them into a second captivity. They could not understand how a God they couldn't see, would choose them and lead them into what seemed to be a trap in the wilderness. Only godly wisdom could help them discern His ways. Why did God use a wilderness for a training ground? It's because His will is always discovered in a wild place.

I believe that God is still active like this in our wildernesses today and this is where He desires to meet with His people. I am not alone with this view. The history of God working in and through the wilderness in the Old Testament is striking and compelling. God chose to start His creation and to start the creation of His chosen people and place them in a garden, a wild place. Jacob fled to the wilderness to be safe from his brother and wrestled with God there, as described in Genesis. God prepared Moses, in the wilderness as he shepherded sheep. David, "the king after God's own heart (1 Sam. 13:14)," was also a shepherd and was also equipped to lead after training in wild places. Elijah, the prophet, was also familiar with the wilderness and went there by himself to rest and recover from his enemies; he also met God there in the wilderness.

In the New Testament, God continues to work and move in the wilderness. John the Baptist preached repentance in the wilderness. Jesus was led by the Spirit into the wilderness. Paul and other disciples traveled through the wilderness as they taught the gospel of God. They were captured, tortured and treated less than human, in some cases, as they went about to speak to the lost children of Israel, who you know as the Gentiles. Therefore, we should not neglect the use of the wilderness as a tool for teaching, learning, and making disciples in our present time. The wilderness helps us with our ability to survive. Survival will make you stronger or make you surrender, depending on how much you value being alive. That drive to survive and stay alive, the love we have to teach our children the difference between right and wrong, the desire to leave some evidence behind that we were here on earth seems to come to us effortlessly. But obedience to God is as hard to learn as trigonometry, (not one of my favorite subjects). So, God has to put us in a place that will teach us His voice and train us how to live a life completely dependent upon Him.

It is in the wilderness that God trains us for battle. It is in the wilderness that we learn how to pray. It is in the wilderness that we learn how to rebuke devils. It is in the wilderness that we learn how to cast out devils. It is in the wilderness that we learn how to cast down vain imaginations. It is in the wilderness that God pulls off our covers and reveals to us who we really are. It is in the wilderness that God performs surgery and cuts away our sins. It is in the wilderness that we learn how to stand boldly for our God. The wilderness you're in could be the dark place that God is using as a cocoon of transformation. You could be gaining enough strength to push through the inner wall and spread your wings. So don't curse your cocoon, caterpillar, God is getting you ready to fly!

How else will you trust Him? How else will you learn patience? To make a way in the wilderness, how else will you learn to seek Him? This is what this book is about. To teach you, and whomever you share this book with, how to live a life that is totally obedient to God. When you look over the history of the Bible you will see that the Israelites were confined to a prepared wilderness with God. Their enemies and the animals God used had to be trained to teach the children of Israel a life of obedience. The Israelites are the chosen people of God so God set everything up to prepare them for a life after the Garden of Eden. My hope is that as you walk through the wilds of these chapters you will use what God has given you for the purpose it was intended and to achieve the unattainable so it can become the touchable. *"It is true that wisdom cries out in the streets but the burden of her cry is to bid us to find her"* (Proverbs 2:1-11). I believe she (wisdom) can be seen in the life of the animal kingdom as well as in the streets of our daily lives.

Now, let's take a journey through the wilderness and watch how the animals obey their God. Without provocation, obedience should be a natural inclination. If you are not a lover of animals, at least take the time to learn how to use what God gave you for the purpose He gave, you'll be wise beyond your years. Watch how the eagle soars above the storm and uses the momentum of the storms clouds to rise. Watch how the ants work together. Though they may not have size and strength they have brains and bravery, proving there is power in numbers. Learn why the lion has the right to rest because he's earned it by battling victoriously for territory. Observe the cleverness of the cheetah, and how feeding her young depends on her taking calculated risks to get close to her prey. Animals' obedience to God says more than you will ever know. That's why this book is important, to show you how your wilderness time can lead you to God.

CHAPTER | SIX

THE WISDOM THAT SOARS

"As an eagle that stirreth up her nest that fluttered over her young He spread abroad his wings, he took them, He bare them on his pinions: The Lord alone did lead him and there was no strange god with him."
- Deuteronomy 32:11:12

The National Eagle Center in Minnesota, MN has one of the highest eagle concentrations. You can see up close a few of the eagles that have been rescued and that are being cared for without cages. I have a special attraction to this particular bird and anyone who spends an afternoon watching them, would easily understand why. These large majestic beings with their earthly colored bodies and heads adorned with the whiteness of experience seem to possess an inherent wisdom and a knowing gaze. If you wish to see an eagle in flight, you must take the time to be thorough and look beyond the places you might expect to see a bird in the sky. Eagles often soar at amazing altitudes and even seem to disappear behind the highest clouds from time to time. When you find an eagle in flight, you quickly notice that eagles are masters of energy conservation. By completely spreading its wings and by paying careful attention to balance, it uses only a minimal expenditure of energy to remain afloat, moving at great speeds, buoyed by the natural currents of air, and trusting that the wind will carry it precisely where it needs to be.

The Children of Israel were trained to worship God — in spirit and in truth. They never saw Him, but every morning they had the best testimonies of His existence. Around the camp laid the manna like dew on the ground when they woke from their slumber. Their feet waxed not weary; neither did their garments become old throughout the years. And before them on their tables, they had constant proof of God's existence by how He cared for them. God led the Israelites every day and in every way while they were in the wilderness, from their cradles to their graves. Moses, being familiar with the wilderness, probably watched eagles many times. It's an intrepid figure of God who said, *"I bare you on eagle's wings and brought you unto myself."*

This illustration teaches us the compassion and strength of God and how He sometimes has to wound you to get you to worship, to break you before blessing you and to shake you while sustaining you at the same time. He teaches us sometimes by His sweet mercy and at other times by bitter affliction. However, before He does any of that He has to get your permission to love you.

God's Tough Love

I want to be very clear that this section is a description of how much God loves Israel. I would say you can compare it to a mother's love for her children or a mother eagle's love for her eaglet. You will get a better understanding of how God administered tough love to Israel because of their constant disobedience. If you don't know the children of Israel went into captivity several times over, Egyptians, other African nations, Grecian, Roman and then here in America because of our continued desires to be like other nations and the constant breaking of His commandments, laws, and statues. The mother eagle shows tough love to her eaglet when she pushes it out of the nest and forces it to fly. The eaglets would never know the mystery of flight sitting in the nest. Tough love is showed when they are pushed from their comforts but the mother eagle knows what's best for the bird. The eaglet's wings are too big for the nest and if they try to stay it becomes problematic, that's why the mother frees the eaglet from their captivity and into their destiny.

We will never know what we can accomplish through our faith in God until we are pushed to flap and fly. God's wisdom and love are given to us under the very poetical picture of the eagle training its young for flight. God, to accommodate Himself to our poor understandings, sometimes compares Himself to a father with children; at other times to a mother with her little ones; sometimes even to an animal.

In this case, a bird of prey, so that we may learn no depths of condescension are too great for God who I am comparing to the eagle.

When God took Israel under His wings, it was for training purposes to teach them that one day, they too would be able to fly. In our quest for promotion and validation we, at times rely, on the success of others to find fulfillment. If this way of thinking is not done away with a person of faith can become a victim of paralysis in a cradle that was only meant to be a place of safety for a short period of time. Looking at the eagle we know that weeks before the eaglets are hatched the eagles begins building a nest. It turns out that the building of an eagles' nest is quite an elaborate affair. A pair of eagles may take up to six weeks to build a nest, in the top of a tree or on the highest mountain. They line it with soft grass, moss, cornstalks, etc., and then it tenderly lines the bottom with feathers (sometimes their own) for comfort. For the first 12 weeks of the young eaglet's life it spends its time relaxing and trusting the parents to provide everything it needs. When it's time for the eaglet to learn to fly, the mother and father collaborate to issue evictions notices. They use their talons to pull apart the soft materials that have been lining the nest. Then the mother eagle rises up and hovers over the nest flapping her wings, stirring the nest. She does all this while all of the comfortable material is being removed by the father.

The message conveyed is it is time to get out of your comfort zone and discover your natural ability to fly. Like the young eagle, many people are guilty of trying to stay in a place of comfort far too long. In these places, God no longer exists because His presence is needed in another place. We prefer lying in the lap of luxury. We like being fed, coddled, and nurtured, that we quickly forget that when God moves out, we should too. Eaglets don't have that luxury because if necessary, the mother will push her baby out of the nest and into the wilderness of survival. The mother knows that her young eagle can fly, but the eaglet has yet to realize the same. In these instances, it takes a stirring on the outside, in hopes that the eaglet will feel the burning on the inside and spread its wings. The burning on the inside is the instinctive inclination to the bird that it was born to soar. Of course, eaglets cannot question the reason why they are being pushed out of its nest but if you are surrounded by comforts and all of a sudden discomfort enters in, you may begin to question God or those around you who have allowed you to remain comfortable for too long.

The Big Push

Here is what happens in between the push and the catch. When the eaglet is old enough to use its wings, it doesn't know it can fly. The mother has to begin training the eaglet for the big push. So let me walk you through the big push. The drop is long and fast. Just as the baby eaglet is about to hit the ground, mother swoops in and catches her young eaglet. This is a scary moment in the life of the eaglet. Not only is it scary but it is a defining moment but up until this juncture in its young life, the eaglet doesn't know when or if its mom will catch it, but she does. It is a lesson in patience, that displays on the screen of life, that you have the fortitude to endure those "big push" moments. If you would admit it, we get pushed around a bit every day. While the workplace, for some, can be a place of peace, for others it's a playground, filled with adult bullies who push us to our limits. The enemy of our souls is very creative in how he manipulates and uses our tools of survival against us. He will use them like heavy moving equipment to push us around like sand in the wilderness. You need that job, but he uses co-workers to push you out of the position you prayed for to get you back in the wilderness of unemployment and thinking that God failed you.

Marriages are challenged to maintain and honor God in ways unimaginable. You've worked so hard to maintain yours in the sight of God but there is a push coming from within your happy home that seeks to drive you out into the wilderness of singleness, sorrow, and loneliness. The pushing may be from the opposing forces but the catching is up to God. He will teach you how, even in complete vulnerability, He can be trusted. The enemy uses everything in his power to make you believe that you have no power in your marriage, on your job, or in other areas of your life. That leaves you fighting against those God placed around you rather than fighting the one who is trying to destroy you. It's a simple trick the enemy uses that messes with your stuff, takes you out of your comfort zone, and keeps you focusing on everything but the goodness of God will help you to seek out obedience diligently.

As the vultures and other predators are hoping the mother will miscalculate the catch, making their meal easy and instant, she displays pinpoint accuracy in catching the eaglet before its body hits the ground. The mothers and fathers of wisdom used to say in the church back then, *"He may not come when you want him but He's right on time!"* And if we could hear the eaglet on the big push method, it would probably testify in a similar way by chirping.

Moses got an opportunity to get to know Jehovah in a way that others had yet to see, especially Israel. If you will read carefully over the history of the children of Israel in the wilderness, I think you will see that God used practical ways of training them. And if they had been obedient followers He wouldn't have had to keep them in the wilderness for 40 years. Here were a people taken away from the multiplicity of gods in Egypt, and now they were being taught to worship an unseen God. They were being trained to worship God spiritually and obediently.

The highlight of Israel's wilderness experience is captured in Exodus. What we don't realize as we read that wonderful chapter is that Israel wasn't lost! Israel was being led by God. God didn't leave His people to find their own way; instead He went before them as a cloud by day and a pillar of fire by night. God was taking Israel through the wilderness for a reason and therefore the wilderness journey wasn't a mistake. God says, "I bore you on eagles' wings," a high expression of the tenderness God had shown for them. It indicates great speed. God not only came upon the wing for their deliverance, but He hastened them out, as it were, upon the wing. He did it with great simplicity, strength, and swiftness of an eagle. It also represents God's particular care and affection to them. Even Egypt, that iron furnace, was like a nest in which they were hatched, where they were first formed as the embryo of a mighty nation of particular people.

As the Israelites increased in numbers, they grew to some maturity, and were carried out of that nest of Egypt. God carried the Israelites out of captivity just like the mother eagle carries her eaglet on her wings until it is ready to totally fly on its own. At the Red Sea, the pillar of cloud and fire moved the Israelites to safety from Pharaoh's army. The presence of God interposed itself between the Israelites and their pursuers, a line of defense which could not be forced or penetrated. That powerful presence seemed to say, "I brought you unto myself." The Israelites were brought not only into a state of freedom but into a covenant with God. He carried them. The eagle carries its young out of harm's way when it realizes their young are not ready or strong enough to fly on its own.

My rhetorical question for you, have you ever been carried by God?

Of course you have! Perhaps the better question is, do you have enough sense to know it was God who was carrying you?

Just like God carries you when you know you have only a little money to last you but you remain obedient to tithing. Just like the time you went to the doctor's office and you received a bad report but when you came back a week or so later and that report is good. Just like the time you were in a bad accident but you walked away with nothing more than a scratch or nothing wrong at all. Just like the time when you applied for a job you didn't qualify for but instead of the position you were instantly promoted to a better job. God gave you every opportunity you have been blessed with because He knew you'd say God did it! He carried you. Perhaps the reason God stirs your nest is because you are trying to rest where God used to be. And that's where the problems start. There's no need to cry in your wilderness. If you embrace the strength of the eagle and learn its wisdom, then you won't waste time with worrying tears.

This is where you should be shouting! This statement means that in your wilderness, if you take the time to pay close attention to where God is taking you and how He is preparing you, then you will know that you will be alright when you come out of your wilderness.

I recall watching a clip from National Geographic that showed an eagle in flight. This great creature miscalculated its descent while trying to catch a fish. The eagle dived too late and ended up falling in the water before it could pull up. Those observing learned that the wings of an eagle are too heavy to flap once they are soaking wet. The eagle had to try and swim to shore, something it is not accustomed to, not to mention that now it has fallen prey to what lies beneath the water. This gives insight to why the eagle is never caught in a storm cloud but always above it. It uses the wind to elevate itself because eagles can't fly with wet wings. Eagles are gracious when they are at their best, above the storm and away from predators who can take them out. That's why God, through the eyes of Moses, leaves a picture of his love for the Israelites when He brought them out of captivity into the wilderness. We, too, can find comfort in knowing that we are related to a sovereign, majestic, and omnipotent God who will one day save us, strengthen us, and restore us just like the eagle and her young.

Open your heart and mind and listen to the eagle speak inside of you. Fly with me and get ready for the unexpected. Stop crying in the storm and start flying above it because there will come a time when God will put you in a place where your life depends on your ability to capture and maintain the power of obedience.

CHAPTER | SEVEN

WISDOM GIVES CHASE

"...as the deer panteth for streams of water."
Psalms 42:1

She's been stalking for hours now and she has her eyes on a small herd of antelope in the field nearby. She can go from nothing to 60 miles per hour in under three seconds. Her elastic spine arches up and down to give her a seven meter stride. For more than half the chase she is airborne. Hurdling at 70 miles per hour, she risks everything on one trip for her prey. She strikes, it trips, and dinner is served.

Why is the Cheetah chasing with so much fervor and determination? Because the lives of her cubs are at stake. Her hungry cubs have been waiting to eat for several days and the internal struggle has forced her to make life altering decisions. Should she stay home and protect her cubs or should she risk it all to face the wild to win them dinner? Catching dinner for her cubs is one thing, but keeping it will be another. Even though she lives in the fast lane, she is only successful if she can get close enough to her prey to give herself a chance at survival. She has great speed and skill but she can only keep it up for 20 seconds. You might think that occupying this specialized niche guarantees her a meal. However, chasing prey and catching it are two different things. The cheetah's body produces glycogen; nature's own rocket fuel. Glycogen is also the same chemical that breaks down into lactate acid and causes muscle cramps. So the female cheetah has just 20 seconds to make her catch before her muscles burn out.

Cheetahs are perfectly adapted for hunting in the grasslands and plains. Being so quick, the cheetah is able to capture prey that no other animals are able to catch. You might say that cheetahs invented fast food because they have to be fast to catch their food. However, getting off to a great start is good in the wild but it doesn't necessarily translate when it comes to walking in obedience to God. Finishing is more important than starting. The fleeing and chasing of the cheetah and her prey is the exact portrait of God chasing His children. He chases us and we get very creative in our attempts to elude His amazing grace. Jesus announced to the church that if anyone thirsts, He has an insatiable drink of water that will satisfy any soul in John 7:37. If there is going to be satisfaction in walking in obedience to God, there will have to be a halt in running long enough to experience the grace of God that gives chase.

When God Chases

This is how God begins chasing us. Jesus once held a small child in His arms and asked his disci ples, *"What do you think? If a shepherd has a hundre d sheep, and one of them has gone astray, does he not le ave the ninety-nine on the mountains and go in search of the one that went astray?"*

With that one scene we get to see how God really values us. He wants us to be humble like children, removed from sin and in innocence purest form, coming to Him with open arms to be held and guided. God, the ruler of the Kingdom of Heaven, chases us down. I know that everyone needs to feel close to other people. It makes us happy to have family and friends who really love, value, and understand us. It's our connection to the world and the belief that we are valuable to others we encounter on a personal level. And just like our need for approval and love from other's God still mercifully searched for Israel everywhere we went. Bondage after bondage, failure after failure, betrayal after betrayal, He longed for us because He created us just for Him… His own people. Even in Hosea—one of the most judgment-heavy books of the Bible—God raises His hand to rain destruction from the heavens on a rebellious Israel but stops Himself at the thought of His love for Israel and the promises He made:

> *"How can I give you up, Ephraim?*
> *How can I hand you over, O Israel?*
> *My heart recoils within me; my compassion grows warm and tender.*
> *I will not execute my fierce anger; I will not again destroy Ephraim; for I am God and no mortal, the Holy One in your midst, and I will not come in wrath.*
> *Many find it hard to believe that God wants to be close to them. They feel they are not worthy of having a relationship with him or that he is too far away. But it is possible to draw close to God because the more we draw nigh unto him he will draw nigh unto us."* (James 4:8)

The Psalmist tells us that *"Surely His goodness and steadfast love will follow all the days of my life."* Psalm 23:6

This phrase tends to translate "will follow me," but all other uses of the root have a connotation of hunting, pursuing, even persecuting. God refused and still refuses to give up on us. Ever. On us, on those who leave the church, on those who have never been part of the community. He refuses to give up on Israel because we are His chosen. He is the God who pursues us relentlessly. Until our last day, He will lighten our steps with love.

How We Should Chase God

The yearning of the Psalmist's soul for communion with God is like a deer panting for a stream of water. The deer has been running for his life for the last 20-30 seconds. Although this doesn't seem like much time, I believe that time slows down dramatically when you see your life flashing before your eyes. It is in this moment of panic and desperation that we can be confident in our will to live because of the wisdom we've gained to survive. One mistake, one misstep, and your life can be over before you know it.

When it comes to serving God, He is not interested in how fast you get started. He's interested in how you finish. Speed comes at a price for the cheetah because she overheats. Overheating or spiritual burnout is a problem for any human testing the limits of faith. Running too fast on your spiritual journey for too long can cause your brain to cook and your spirit to burnout. You try too hard to absorb as much knowledge as you can that you can easily confuse yourself on which direction you are heading when it comes to your relationship with God. Here's what I know when it comes to the cheetah, she has a solution to not burning out or overheating. She knows her speed comes with limited range. So she knows exactly what she wants and decides when and how she will attack it. This is why God gives Israel instructions on how to keep His commandments. It is important that you are consecrated and connected to God because walking in obedience cannot be done in your own strength. The good news is God gives us help. The rule is simple:

Obey and you will be blessed!

The cheetah has to be obedient to her hunger, to the need to feed her young, and to the overall need to survive. And when the heat is on, it's all about timing. It all depends on who gets a head start. That split second timing is tested over and over with varying degrees of success depending, of course, on whose view you choose. It's on these vast grasslands where predators and prey play out their life and death struggles. This is the same place where a wayward nation of Israel was taught the meaning of a close relationship with God.

Always remember we are Israel!

The day Israel was set free from Egypt was a day of exhilaration, anticipation, and initial obedience. However, when the difficulties came, the excitement they demonstrated diminished along the way. It seems to me that something happened that led them to disobedience during their journey. Whatever they had at the start disappeared during the chase. I think what happened to the nation of Israel is exactly what happens in the life of the believer. The desire to be independent from God while attaching themselves to the standards or other nations is what led the national of Israel to disobedience.

During the journey, the joy of their freedom was overruled by the seduction of complacency. Israel began to get comfortable enough in the wilderness that they began to complain about their leader to an unknown God. They then complained to an unknown God about an unqualified leader, Moses. Comfort, without control, leads to noncompliance or, in other words, disobedience. So, let's take a quick journey back to Israel in the wilderness…

After the Israelites got out of Egypt they journeyed on a path that brought them to the

Wilderness of Sinai. It took them three months of trusting Moses, who was God's representative, to get to that place, but they arrived. They saw God's deliverance from Egypt; they received His guidance on the way; and saw His glorious victory won over the Amalekites. But, they were not yet where they needed to be spiritually. For some it would take a while, for others they would never make it to the Promised Land because of excessive disobedience. However, a few would learn the lesson they would be taught in the incubator of the wilderness.

Israel stayed in the Wilderness of Sinai from Exodus until Numbers 10. More than 57 chapters of biblical scriptures are devoted to what happened to Israel in the year they camped at Mount Sinai. The word conventionally translated "wilderness" is not a sandy desert, but grazing country, not developed by man. So Israel camped there before the mountain. In one sense, all that went before was meant to bring them to this place. This was the beginning of the fulfillment of what God said in Exodus 3:12, *"This shall be a sign to you that I have sent you: When you have brought the people out of Egypt, you shall serve God on this mountain."*

Sinai was the place where Moses met God at

the burning bush. The whole nation of Israel would soon experience some of what Moses did at the burning bush. What they needed to learn at Sinai was a lesson we can and should use today. When you decide to follow God, get close to Him and stay close to Him. The need to get close to God is one that will enhance every aspect of our lives for the rest of our lives when we understand its importance. I want you to know that if God is going to be your God, you will need a close relationship with Him.

In the wilderness of Sinai, there are so many uncertainties and a way of living that is uncommon to recent and former slaves of Egypt. The pecking order has been established. In essence, God says, *"You are in the wilderness. You don't know where you're going, what danger there is out here. I am your God and I will lead you through this great wilderness. If you obey me you will be blessed. If you fail to obey me you will be cursed."* Diggs translation of Deut. 28:13.

So they camped in the wild grazing country and while in the wilderness, the nation of Israel shared it with whatever made the wild its home. With instructions from God, there's a lot to be learned from the beasts of the field. And as they're settling and meditating on the words God told to them through Moses. They had to listen intentionally to Moses when he came back with a word from God. But some mumbled and grumbled because they missed the captivity that kept them with a certain condition that they no longer had in the wilderness. You see, they didn't have to hunger for anything because they were guaranteed to get just enough to stop the hunger when they were in Egypt.

I wonder how anyone can miss the hardships of slavery or lack when God has promised them better. They just needed to be prepared in the wilderness.

If we look closer at the cheetah, then we see her and her cubs moving in the nearby bush. Apparently, the mother is preparing to leave her cubs because they need something to eat. The growl in her stomach forces her from her dwelling place. She has her eye on a herd of antelope in the distance but inside this cheetah is an internal struggle (instincts) she can't escape. She has speed, she has skill, she has sharp teeth but she lacks endurance. She can outperform a Porsche on the freeway but she can only keep up that speed for about 20 seconds. She has no problem getting out the gate but it's the finish that usually does her in. The one and only thing that she knows is it is time for her to survive. She listens to her instincts that God put in her and she is obedient every time she engages in chasing her prey. She has to listen or she will die.

Israel can learn a divine lesson if they pay attention to this wild animal. They, too, got out of the gate fast when they left Egypt in a hurry. Two million people got out of Egypt in about 40 minutes. They left with what they had and what most don't realize is that some of the Egyptians traveled with them, I'll talk about that in a second. Unfortunately, getting out is never the problem. The problem is staying close to who got you out because with freedom comes the temptation to stray. They never saw all of the miracles that was presented to them once they exited Egypt. They witnessed the parting of the Red Sea; they witnessed being fed manna from Heaven; so many miracles but they were never satisfied. Part of me believes it's because it's in our human nature to never be satisfied. But, it could be because we had other nations whispering in our ears telling us that we should expect no demand more. They could have been successful and fulfilled the void that was growling in their stomachs if they had more of a desire and need for a close relationship with God through Moses.

Just like the cheetah's success depends on if she can get close enough to her targeted prey without being seen to pounce on the catch of the day and bring it home, Israel's success depends on if they can maintain the fervor for Jehovah they once had. If we are going to make sound decisions that determine whether we live or die, we must get close to God and stay there. To compare cheetahs to Christians in that they both lack endurance after taking off would be stating the obvious. Many Christian converts get out of the gospel gate fast with enthusiasm and give up in a few months when they don't catch the breaks and blessings they think they deserve. However, walking by faith is more like slow cooking a roast than scrambling an egg. Some Christians just do not have the staying power. They only last for a short time and then fall away, back into the same world they were fleeing from.

Endurance, however, is only a part of the struggle that a cheetah faces as wells as new converts. In observing the hunt, chase, and catch of the cheetah and its prey, there are similar crucial steps needed to attain the wisdom necessary to lay hold of God's grace. If you'd observe the brief chase and catch of the cheetah, you would see the steps needed to catch hold of

God. The cheetah recognizes the first step in getting closer to God is simply to know the truth about her ability and her prey. The truth the cheetah knows it that she is quick, stealth but she is not a fighter. She must know her weaknesses and her strengths. Attempting to take down a buffalo would be futile. Attempting to chase down a rabbit would be insufficient. So, she crouches and waits until she is confident enough in her ability to commit to the chase.

Drawing nearer to God for us means getting lower. It is humbling yourself under the Word of God. In James 4:8 it states, *"Draw nigh to God, and he will draw nigh to you. Cleanse your hands, ye sinners; and purify your hearts, ye double minded."* Isaiah 55:6 states, *"Seek ye the Lord while he may be found, call ye upon him while he is near:"*

People will make the statement of not feeling close to God but never humble themselves enough to admit they hadn't made Him their top priority. Feelings of disconnect and alienation and wondering if God even heard you doesn't always means something is wrong with you. Sometimes, a person needs to admit that God was not the most important part of their life. Also, it is important to understand that when you are not being obedient to God's word, you are not a priority to Him either. John 9:31 proves this point, *"Now we know that God heareth not sinners: but if any man be a worshipper of God, and doeth his will, him he heareth."* That simply means if you are not living according to the word of God and you are constantly placing Him on the back burner then He will not hear you.

Reading the truth of God's word will always reveal the truth about who you really are. This will let you know if what you are chasing is actually worth keeping. Know your strengths and weaknesses by knowing the truth of who God is to you and what He has in store for you. Jesus said in John 8:32, *"And ye shall know the truth and the truth shall make you free."*

I want to offer you three steps when establishing a lasting relationship with God. Not a fleeting one that you're not committed to but one that demands your undivided attention without fail:

- Have a moment of consecration.
- Take a calculated risk.
- Make a commitment to chase.

Have a Moment of Consecration

When you take time to realize that you need God just as much as He needs you then you will be able to have a moment of consecration. God is like a father or mother waiting for their child to bring home a report card. The parents have taught their child everything they need to know about learning and being a good student. So when the report cards come home they expect and anticipate straight As or even A's and B's. So, the parent is eager in seeing the exemplary success of the student. But oh how the parent is disappointed when their child brings home less than good grades. The disappointment they face when they see the report card that reflect poor behavior and grades is great. There are two things that can happen. The parent can blame the student for not trying or blame the teacher.

Unfortunately, there are some parents who do the latter. They refuse to accept the truth that their child may not be applying the skills and lessons they have been taught. But God sees you and what you are not doing when it comes to getting closer to Him. He knows that you are not studying your Bible. He knows you are preoccupied with everything else when it is time for you to hear His word. He knows that your best efforts are not as good as they should be. He doesn't blame the pastor (your teacher) because God knows that accountability starts with you.

You!

You have to get to a place in which you have a true hunger for God and not a needy hunger for Him. That needy hunger comes when you want Him to bless your mess or you want Him to handle your enemies. You know how you have done sometimes, made God your ABM… automatic blessing machine. Your desire to be obedient to God has to be such a commitment that you know if you don't do it, it will literally mean being blessed, shaken down, stirred together and running over. You have to be committed to being obedient and not obligated. There is a difference.

A Calculated Risk

A calculated risk is an intentional act of aggression. It is also a necessary step in pursuing a relationship with God. Going back to the cheetah, it has to make up in her mind if this is a catch worth pursuing. If it's too big, then it's too risky. If it's too small, then it will be insufficient for her and her cubs. So she finds a secret place to stop and think. She's a consecrated feline. Before she uses her God given ability she has to have this conversation with herself.

"With my limited amount of endurance, is what I'm chasing worth the effort?" She's asking herself if "THIS" catch is "THE" catch.

God told Israel before they get too far into the journey to make up your mind if I'm worth pursuing. You can see Him clearly giving them an option in Exodus 19:10, "*And the Lord said unto Moses, Go unto the people, and sanctify them to day and to morrow, and let them wash their clothes…*" In essence, He was telling them to separate themselves, sanctify themselves, and consider if God is worth obeying. The time is always right for you and me to ask ourselves, "What has God done for me?" "Are His commandments too hard to follow?" "Is His love to unreal to accept?" "Is his grace insufficient?"

The answer is of course, no. God is ALWAYS worth the risk. There's a taste in your mouth that only God can satisfy. It's telling your heart and your stomach that God is all you need. Will you obey your hunger or starve contemplating how to find other ways to fulfill you need?

A Commitment to the Chase

As the whipping grass stings her eyes it is mainly the sound of her target that she depends on during the chase. The problem is not running, sometimes the problem is lack of commitment to the chase. She is the fastest land mammal and can run up to speeds of 70 mph. However, obstacles and past disappointments can steal her confidence before the chase. Sometimes, what we don't have overshadows what we can have if only we would make the commitment. It's not that you can't serve; it's whether or not you are committed to serving. It's not that you can't sing a solo on Sunday; it's whether or not you are committed to choir rehearsals. It's not that you can't lead; it's whether or not you are committed to being led. It's not what you don't have that hinders you. The question is, will you commit to what you do have? You will never conquer what you will not commit to.

The stony soil, in the parable of the sower, represents such a person who starts off in the faith but fizzle after a while. Of the four soils in the parable, one was stony. The seed which fell on this soil immediately sprang up (Matthew 13:5). Later, Jesus explained the parable and pointed out specifically that the seed which fell on the stony place represents one who hears the Word and receives it immediately with joy. He also said, "yet he has no root in himself, but endures only for a while" (NKJV). This person started well but due to difficulties, fell away.

An Olympic sprinter would have real problems trying to keep up with a cheetah. With all of its speed, however, the cheetah just cannot run fast for very long. Sadly, in a similar way, many have no endurance in their service to God. They start with the speed of a cheetah but they don't last. We must have perseverance in serving God. Hebrews 10:23 says, *"Let us hold fast the confession of our hope without wavering, for He who promised is faithful."*

You can't rush the chase and you can't lose sight of your target, but you can commit to the chase because when the moment presents itself - life depends on immediate execution. If you get close to God, then it is never an accidental occasional thing. If you are close, then it is because you intended to get close to God. Drawing close to God is not something that just happens because you have given your life to Christ and you made the decision to start going to church.

When a person has gotten close to the Almighty it's because they were trying to. And the reason the cheetah doesn't just pop out of the bushes and start chasing is because she has to tiptoe, crouch, crawl and pretend she isn't looking in order to get close. She'll even play possum, a classic game of cat and mouse. However, what looks like a game has been given to her as a strategy for success. God has a strategy for us to be closer to Him. It's almost as if He is playing cat and mouse with us because He allows us to chase everything and everyone else and when we are tired and feeling lost He is there waiting to snatch us back into His loving grace.

The God we see in the scriptures, from Genesis to Revelation, is one who loves despite. Despite our sin, our waywardness, our piety, our efforts, our failures, despite everything. From the complaining under Moses to the rejection of God as King, from idolatry under the monarchs to the compromise under the Romans, Greeks and Persians God across thousands of years has pursued a stubborn people called Israel.

When all else fails, He appears in the flesh to knock on their doors, to sleep in their gardens, to eat at their tables and to call them back to Him.

God will not let them go. It is here that we find our hope. We hope to one day have the same devotion from the God of Israel that even when it seems that we have crossed the final line, we see God, shepherd staff in hand, come rushing over the hill to bring us back. And how ecstatic are we when this becomes a reality? When God makes a way for us to become part of the chosen people through the death and resurrection of Christ? We are now a part of the flock, part of the one hundred. Should even one of us—any one of us—go astray, the Shepherd will begin His chase again. That's why Jesus asked the disciples in the parable about the lost sheep and coin. Though it seems there are many to still be had, is it not important to go find the one that is lost. Yes, God cares that much for us that He does everything He needs to do to bring us back to us love.

The cheetah, when it's time, will use all of her energy to bring the prey she chose to run down back to her cubs. That's the entire agenda why she went out to hunt… to feed her natural body and to feed her cubs. We have to know that when we run away from Christ, He will bring us back to Him. We maybe burden heavy and grief stricken but we know that once we regain our energy we will be wiser and stronger.

CHAPTER | EIGHT

THE WISDOM TO WORK IT OUT

"A man's got to do what a man's got to do, but a woman has got to do what he can't."
– Rhonda Hansome

The king of the jungle always gets the attention. We know more about him because of his powerful attacking skills, because of his wonderful land full mane, because, well he is the king of the jungle. However, shouldn't we spend some time looking at the power behind the throne that is the queen of the jungle? Lisa Bevere, author of *Lioness Arising: Wake Up and Change Your World*, believes we should.

Women should be like the lioness, beautiful. One of the definitions of beauty in Webster's dictionary is "a beautiful person, especially a woman."

I would agree when we think of beauty in a person we generally think of women; however we can see beauty in the actions of any person, male or female. The Bible has much to say about the beauty of women. Beautiful women may be defined as such because of physical features, but in the Bible we see more about beauty as defined by character. The Proverbs 31 woman teaches about the ideal woman. She is powerful. She is strong. She is nurturing. She is stunning and she has strength.

I believe if you look through the eyes of faith at the lioness, you will find remarkable success in the midst of her daily struggles. The wilderness gives us wisdom from on high from the lovely lioness. Her willingness to survive is greater than whatever wants her dead. One of the most important jobs of a lioness is to protect her cubs. Unfortunately, 40 to 80 percent of lion cubs die before their first year, either by starvation or coalition. For this reason, mother is always in a bad mood. She has to deal with the constant dilemma of getting dinner to feed her cubs or remaining close to the den in order to protect them. Each day she stays home is a day closer her cubs starving to death. She has to protect, nurture and hunt for her cubs. She is consumed by the demands that have been placed upon her life. The Lioness is a good mother. Every cub deserves an equal chance of survival. Every cub needs to be protected, nurtured, trained and provided for.

She's raising a cub while serving the king. So that means she is always on edge, but she's always prepared for the next battle because her sisters have her back. She has a pride that she can depend on because they have learned the art of cooperative hunting. Seven out of ten lioness' hunts result in failure when she hunts alone, but when lioness' hunt together, the success rate increases to 90 to 100 percent. To bring down prey three or four times their size they will need cooperation. Life and death for the pride relies on togetherness.

Can I talk to you lioness?

Don't fight your sisters for position. You should be fighting together for possession. Whether single or married, you are the queen of what you can control. The lioness has killer instincts and a nurturing touch. In order to protect their young from wandering and invading lions to raising their young, the lioness relies on protection from their resident males. Hunting for a male lion is an unwritten contract that says as long as the dominant male promises to protect the pride, the females will reward him with the first of every catch at meal time. In return the male provides protection, giving the females the sanctuary needed to raise their young.

The reason she hunts for the male is because he has conquered the territory for the pride to hunt. The queen will kill for her king if he creates an environment suitable for hunting. If he takes care of the home and keeps the enemies away, she will put her life on the line while hunting for him and his cubs. In this instance she is a leader because she knows that if she is ever met with a larger foe her king has her back.

Ladies, I want you to re-read that section again.

What I want you to know is, until the lioness finds her king, she can be a fugitive in her own land. So, in summation, a brief overview of the life of a lioness can provide assistance in your wilderness of society. Here are some qualities that I believe are closely related to a woman who is searching for a relationship with Christ when she is in her wilderness.

A lioness is a strong and powerful creature.

The lioness is at ease with her strength and at rest with her power. They are powerful hunters but they spend much of their time in rest and play. Women are the same. If you limit yourself with fear of your own power, then you forfeit your strength and beauty. When you stop struggling in your own ability then you are able to reveal your true strength.

Embrace your strength. Do not mistake meekness for weakness. It is tempered strength and controlled might.

The Lioness sets aside former limitations.

She often fails when she first learns to hunt but that doesn't mean she will never hunt again. Hardship is a catalyst for improvement. You may fail at your first attempts to develop strength, but this is part of the learning process. Accept your failures as stepping stones to your strength and future successes.

The Lioness is stunning.

A lioness is a beautiful creature. She moves with purpose. She is aware that the survival of her pride depends on her kills and strength. Women of every shape, size and color are as stunning, wild, and as fierce as the lioness. There is incredible beauty in the strength of a godly woman. You are capable of incredible things. Recognize this and revel in it. Esther, in the book of Esther, reveled in her beauty as a youth and used her beauty and meekness to capture the heart of the Persian King. She didn't overstate and demand that she be looked upon with ah and wonder. Instead when the time came she used her beauty and the love that her king had for her to save her people, the Israelites.

The Lioness has prowess.

Lionesses are the height of hunting prowess. Their ability to provide for their pride is unmatched. Like the lioness, women too have prowess. There is exceptional ability, strength or valor waiting to be developed in every woman's life. You may not know or do everything, but what you do know, you chose to do well. Ruth, another biblical woman of God uses her prowess to capture the attention of Boaz. He owned the land that Naomi told Ruth to work in. As she worked Boaz ensured that she was taken care of, more than the other workers. Eventually Naomi sent Ruth to lie at the feet of Boaz and from there she was rewarded with marriage to him. She was able to stand out because of her willingness to submit, even to Naomi and to work hard in the fields without complaint.

The Lioness lives in the light.

When a lioness isn't hunting, she has no reason to move about in the shadows. She conducts her life in the open, sun-filled expanses of Africa. She feels no shame and no need to hide. Like the lioness, women must live their lives in the open with a light-filled heart to serve God. You, alone, have the power to open your life to sunlight and live without fear or shame of who you are in Christ. Don't put away who you are, feeling like others will not accept you. Live according to 2 Timothy 1:7, *"For God hath not given us the spirit of fear; but of power, and of love, and of a sound mind."* In biblical history God often called upon a woman to do what men could not do because they doubted Him. Be used by God in the light of His word.

Lionesses roar.

When the cubs are threatened, the lionesses will roar as a group in a fearless proclamation of protection. Women must also be a voice for the voiceless. You must learn to live that which is within you and live out loud. All the intangibles of faith, hope and love become tangibles throughout the world. There's much wisdom in the wild to be gained from the lioness. Max Lucado states, "A woman's heart should be so hidden in God that a man has to seek Him just to find her."

Learn from the lioness, women of God.

She'll stay low, she'll stay submissive, but she will never back down. Don't be afraid of your strength, questions, or insights. Awaken, rise up and dare to realize all you were created to be. You were born for this moment.

CHAPTER | NINE

WISDOM IS CULTIVATED

"Like newborn babies, long for the pure milk of the word, so that by it you may grow in respect to salvation . . ."

- I Peters 2:2

Grilled cheese sandwiches after school are a tradition in the Diggs' home. Our son, J.R., longs for a grilled cheese as soon as he hits the door from school. One afternoon, while I was washing the pan after making him a grilled cheese sandwich, I found myself admiring the sponge I was using to clean the pan. There is normally a brief glance after I squeeze the water out but this day, it caught my attention.

Sponges have always intrigued me. There is something about their appearance, feel and absorptive qualities that is most fascinating to me. It was with a great deal of interest that I went to the internet and did a little research on the sponge. I learned in my brief study that sponges are actually animals, and must be cleaned before they are useful for household purposes. All the living matter must be removed so that the skeleton which remains, with its open-celled structure, can soak up and absorb other elements.

I thought to myself, sponges are a lot like children. They, too, quietly and silently soak up everything with which they come in contact. They are what they are. Not only because of the inheritance of certain characteristics and traits received from their parents, but also because of their environment. As I watched my son finish his snack I began to think of how important it is to be very careful of what is allowed to fill the hearts and minds of our children. How important it is to govern and control their surroundings. It is so important that God, after the Exodus, devoted a passage of scripture on how to cultivate our offspring.

If you are reading this book and you are blessed with a child, consider it a high honor that God has entrusted such a precious life in your hands.

In Deuteronomy 6:7 it says, *"And thou shalt teach them diligently unto thy children, and shalt talk of them when thou sittest in thine house, and when thou walkest by the way, and when thou liest down, and when thou risesth up."* Basically it is important for you to talk about God and the Bible with your children. You have to cover them with the word of God so that they know the will of God. Life is already challenging for children today, which is why we must do our part to keep them close to God as much as we can. God used Moses to talk to His children. Of course God knew that they would complain about everything and anything. He knew that when He brought them out of Egypt that they were going to be a mess. He also knew that with that many traveling children, there would need to be order and rules while journeying through the wilderness. There are always rules in the wild that even the most dangerous killers obey.

Take for instance the lioness. She has been given the task that no other feline in the wild has. She hunts, submits, and serves the king while raising her cubs. Female lions give birth to up to four cubs at a time although litters of two or three are more common. Mothers of young cubs spend most of their time away from the pride, although they may join their companions for brief periods. Cubs are usually hidden in dense bushes for approximately six weeks until they are old enough to join the pride. During the six weeks the cubs rely entirely on their mother looking after them and feeding on their mother's milk.

Occasionally, if the mothers are unable to provide for her cubs, she will abandon them. Mothers must remain in top condition in order to provide for their cubs and caring for cubs at their own expense would likely mean death for both. Her hope is that one day, the wisdom and training she gives her cub will be enough for him to earn a pride of his own. Cubs and adolescent lions are like young teenagers, awkward, eager and easily distracted. Life lessons are constantly before them, but if they fail to learn, then life becomes far more difficult than it should be. If a lion cub doesn't learn then the lesson of hunting and surviving, their future prey could elude them. If the cub is not a careful observer, then opportunities to rule the wild will slip through his paws before he's ever crowned a king.

The lion cub's first responsibility is to know himself. He must learn quickly that his bloodline is important. He has to soon realize that even as a cub he is still a king. Because the cubs are born completely helpless, the lioness keeps them hidden until they begin to learn. The lion cub must soon realize soon that every animal in the wilderness wants him dead based on his potential. As a cub, he is no threat but as soon as he realizes the power and authority he possesses, he will be able to destroy what could have destroyed him as a cub. Though he may be cute, there is a killer on the inside. He's a cub with killer instincts that have not yet been cultivated.

His mother knows his potential. The mother protects her cubs by isolating them from the other male lions. Cubs are born in a dangerous environment. Lion cubs are vulnerable to predators, such as hyenas and leopards, but the most significant threat comes from other male lions. When a new male coalition takes over a pride they are often confronted by the cubs of the males that were defeated. Since females will not mate again until their cubs are 18 months of age, the new males kill all the young cubs in their new pride in order to bring the females back to estrus. Older cubs and sub adult lions only stand a chance if they are able to escape. These cubs are evicted and have to fend for themselves. There are also times when their mothers leave with them and remain apart from the pride until their cubs react independently. While young males are expelled from the pride by the age of three, females usually remain with the pride for their whole lives. So the mother takes the lion cub away from the pride to protect it from infanticide and larger predators that see them as future threats.

Far too often childhood ends for so many of our young people and they'll discover that it's time to make their own way in the world just like the lion cub. The lifelong search for food and survival begins. As is true in the animal kingdom, in the early years of childhood parents must make almost all the decisions. One of the terribly tragic things about life today is the degree to which many parents let children make decisions they are incapable of making.

Focus on the Kids

For wisdom to be king in our lives and the lives of our children, it must be cultivated at an early age.

What do we teach our kids?

Deuteronomy has the answer for those in the wilderness and Ephesians has the answer for those in the Promised Land. In the wilderness states to …impress them on your children. (Deuteronomy 6:7) Unfortunately, like the Israelites in the wilderness, many people are homeless. No, I am not talking about people who are on the street; I am speaking of people who have houses, but not a home. Too often, we could just as well have hotel rooms, a place to sleep and change clothes before heading out the next morning, rather than having the homes we've been blessed with.

A home is built upon relationships with our family. This is done by spending time with your family, sitting down together and actually talking. Our conversations need to be about the goodness of God and the importance of serving Him with our lives. Children learn about the importance of having a personal relationship with God from observing their parents.

There was once a story told of a little girl who went to school. The teacher announced on the first day that she was an atheist (don't believe in God). She asked how many of the children were atheists. All but one little girl raised their hands in order to please their teacher. The teacher focused on the one little girl. She proclaimed that she was a Christian.

The teacher asked, "Why?"

The little girl responded, "Because of my parents."

Teacher sought to embarrass the little girl and asked, "If your parents were morons, what would you be?"

The girl said, "I guess I would be an atheist like you."

Make your house a home and take time to talk with your children about the importance of trusting Christ as their Savior. Don't just tell them, but take the time to show them. Show them from God's word how much God loves them. So, much that He sent His only begotten Son, Jesus to die on Calvary for their sins.

When Thou Walkest in the Way

This is a reference to our day-to-day activities. Children need to see Christ in our lives on a daily basis. Jesus Christ is not just our Savior on Sundays. He is our Savior every day of our lives. Take advantage of the time you spend with your children doing everyday tasks to teach them of God and His Word. This is better than formal education. One of the problems with school is that we are often trying to teach children when they aren't ready to learn. If we as parents take advantage of daily teaching opportunities, then both we, and our children, will benefit greatly. That's why we have to consider the multitude of questions that open the door to teaching about God's grace and goodness. Here are some questions that your child may ask you as they are discovered the world around them:

1. Why is the sky blue?
2. Why is the grass green?
3. Why does the rain fall?
4. Why do the birds sing?
5. How does the wind blow?
6. Where do the clouds go?

These questions, and many more, will always give us an opportunity to open our Bibles and to not only read how God created everything and what He has done for us but it also gives us an opportunity to show our children where it comes from. This is the foundation of building a love and dependency of God that we often miss as we raise our children.

When Thou Liest Down

There is something very special about these times with your children. I loved to watch my older children as they slept. Bedtime is a wonderful opportunity to talk with them about the events of the day. Oftentimes my children would take this time to share their thoughts or spiritual concerns during the day because I was so busy with or that. So, bedtime was their time and that's when I got the really good questions that they were holding in all day. In those times I was able to quiet the storms they were facing at school or the fears they had. That was our perfect time to pray and to share the promises of God's Word. I encourage you to use bedtime as a time to settle your thoughts and allow yourself to be opened to helping your children learn more about God and His goodness.

Psalms 4:8 says, *"I will both lay me down in peace, and sleep: for thou, LORD, only make me dwell in safety."* We have to give our children that moment to feel safe.

When Thou Riseth Up

Getting up on the wrong side of the bed can impact our entire day. Of course we know that it isn't so much whether it is right side or left side. However, that saying has to do with our attitude in the morning. Some will say that they just aren't morning people, but that is just an excuse isn't it?

Mornings are a great time to encourage and teach our children. How we begin each morning can influence the course of the day for our children and ourselves.

The Promised Land

One of the strongest scriptures in the Bible that relates to children is *"Children obey your parents that it may be well with you, and that you may live long on the earth,"* in Ephesians 6:1 NIV. This is a verse that many parents have used over the years to get their children to submit biblical correction with their wayward child. Whatever the reason for the use this scripture has so much power.

As you may recall earlier in chapter 10, the lioness or wife as I call her, submits to her king or husband. The Greek translation hupotasso means equal submission. Paul changes the word here and uses the word that does not apply to the wives, hupakouo. That means inferior. Now in God's eyes children are equal. However, in the family they are inferior and are to submit to a superior, which are the father and mother. You see, there are a lot of families that aren't Spirit-filled. They are dysfunctional. What is wrong? You've got a wife submitting to her husband and a husband loving his wife as Christ loved the church then you might have a child who says, "I'm not going to do it your way, I'm going to do it my way."

Dysfunctional families are usually the result of one or more parties involved ignoring the wisdom of God. There is either failure to teach from the parent or the refusing to listen and learn on the part of the child. Either one can result in damaged relationships and possibly even death.

Consider the question of obedience in the life of a teenager. This is a volatile period of human growth. The child is becoming an adult and seeks to establish autonomy as an individual. This adolescence is often marked by rebellious attitudes toward authority, particularly their parents. Parents find this a very testing time which calls on all their resources of wisdom and patience. Parents with a more mature wisdom and with an eye to the general wellbeing of their child will set limits to the freedom their child seeks.

By the way, what are your children absorbing in your home these days? What are they getting from that television set? What enters those young minds through those magazines on your reading table? In listening to your conversation, what kind of words and attitudes are being impressed upon them? Are good examples being set by your love for the Lord and concern for others? Is there a warm, spiritual emphasis in your home? Are you doing what you can to fill their hearts with God's Word?

In years to come those children will "give out" only that which has been absorbed during their formative, impressionable years. Make sure those little "sponges" in your home soak up only that which is pure, wholesome, and uplifting. Children seldom misquote. They repeat, word for word, what you SHOULD NOT have said. They must learn they are created to be kings and queens in the truth of the word of God.

CHAPTER | TEN

WHEN WISDOM IS KING

"…the righteous are as bold as a lion."
-Proverbs 28:1

At one point in my spiritual quest, while I was in my wilderness, I read the Bible, cover to cover, in one year. I read over many interesting verses that I am now discovering with great joy and enthusiasm. The verse I am about to share with you I hold near and dear to my heart:

Proverbs 28:1, "The righteous are bold as a lion."

That year was the first time I had taken notice of this verse from the word of God and I want to share some of its greatness with you. What I learned when I read that scripture is God's people are to be as bold as lions. We are to be fearless and to live a life that shows we are as such. However, as I looked around at some of the people I was around, and even within my congregation, I was seeing a people who were lost and who were living fearfully. Not fearlessly.

I must have read that scripture a million times and I wondered, what is it about a lion that we should see in our lives as righteous people? Surely, not the growl or the roar of the lion, although many believers think that noise is a sign of power. However, I do believe, the word of God would like for us to adopt the confidence and courage that the lion possesses.

The lion is the king of the beasts.

He has confidence.

He is not afraid of any other animal, and when he is hungry, he will go after anything.

Since he was a cub, he was aware of his kingly status. As a cub, he was constantly attacked by bigger predators. Often hidden by his mother, he may have moved from den to den, in her attempts to keep him alive. He inherited the enemies of his parents in the wild. Yet, after every life threatening episode in battle, whether bruised, beaten, or battered, he is still a king.

This is what God intended for man when he created him in his own image. A man! The head of the household, ruling over territory, conquering would-be challengers while retaining his throne. However, somewhere in the wilderness, it seems that man lost the drive to be king.

My question is why?

"For what is stronger than a lion, or more courageous and undaunted? It walks with great

majesty, very slowly, step by step, the left foot first; shaking its shoulders as it goes without fear, and turneth not away for any." Proverbs 30:30.

A lion does not go out of its way for any creature it meets nor does it hasten its pace when pursued. This creature is an emblem of Christ, the Lion of Judah, who is stronger than the strongman armed who never turned His back to any of His enemies, nor turned aside from the way of His duty. Christ walked fearlessly in His purpose to die so that the children of Israel be restored unto God. He knew the plans of God to be a living sacrifice to fulfill, not destroy, the laws of God. Jesus the Christ pursued His purpose, like a lion pursues its prey. Without fear, but with boldness and majesty walking into a certain uncertainty with one thing on His mind, to obey the will of His father.

In order for wisdom to be king it must be kept behind the fences of its own experiences. The lion cannot be a fox, and the fox cannot be a lion. He can only be what he was created to be. He cannot teach what he doesn't know and he cannot lead where he doesn't go. The lion knows his role and he walks in his purpose abundantly and purposefully. He never sees other animals and wishes to be them because he knows that he is king.

Still, our wonderful God made man to have dominion over everything, even over the most feared of all animals, the lion. Unfortunately, dominion over all things causes us to forget that every animal and creeping thing and bird of the air has a purpose and place. I believe this to be so in order to teach us God's love and how to be obedient. However the man, at times, seems to lack the boldness of the lion. Boldness is the one thing that is lacking among Christians today. Most do not act like a lion. They seem almost afraid, at times, to let people know they are Christians. They slink away when asked questions about the Bible, their church, or even living for the Most High. They become mumbled and oftentimes offended by the thought of persecution for standing boldly in the word of God. Yet the Word says, "the righteous are bold as lions."

So I ask you, "How is this boldness manifested?"

Remember, that first wonderful day when you realized all that was available to you in Christ? When you decided, by an act of your will, to accept it? Did you feel like jumping up and down with joy? Perhaps you jumped for joy inside, but it is not how high you jump but how straight you walk that is important after that.

The night before Jesus was crucified Peter said, *"I will not deny you even though everybody else will know not me" (Matthew 26:33).*

This was a display of boldness by Peter. It was a display of brashness on his part that he may have said it with his lips but when it came time of testing he did not stand. As Christ predicted, Peter denied his relationship with Him so much so that others who had seen him with Christ stood and pointed Peter out. Still he denied Christ. Peter's intentions were bold and his heart may have been bold, but his actions were anything but bold. Instead he denied. I can imagine that Peter was not being tested by his actions because Christ told him that he was the rock that the church would be built on. Maybe Peter was being boldly obedient to his fear of persecution so he could be bold when it was his time to spread the gospel.

Boldness means taking charge. It is shown when you're weak, desperate, or in a tight spot. If there ever was a time for the man to stand up and take charge like the lion it is now! As God spoke to Adam in the Garden, and Moses in the wilderness, I would like to speak to the men reading this book as it comes to a close. The wisdom of the lion cannot be based on desperation. You'll need it all the times, if wisdom will be your king. You need to discern and listen to what God is actually telling you. You have to know when God is saying move towards victory and when He is offering you another route. That can be hard to do but here are some tips I have used to be bold like a lion.

King of His Surroundings

Kings are the most powerful people or rulers of a land. Perhaps this is why the lion is considered king, because it is in control of the land it lives on and all the other animals that live on it. The male lion patrols well-worn paths making sure his presence is felt. He keeps invaders out of their territories by patrolling, marking and roaring, and they will also fight if they encounter a strange male within their territory

Men, we were created to take over territory and lead!

Most men would rather stay out of the way and let the women take the lead but that philosophy was only designed to work in hunting for food. Not saying that your wives go out and hunt for food but in the sense of the lioness she knows her role is to get the food and take care of the cubs. She doesn't worry about fighting predators, unless they are attacking her cubs. Your wives shouldn't have to fight to take care of their homes while you are present. They should be able to take care of the home without worrying about the intrusion of a predator. That predator can be another woman outside of the home, a job that takes you away more than necessary, or friends who do not understand who you are as king in your home.

Men, you have to make sure your presence is felt in your land. That means being at home with your family. In the home we must be priests. In the workplace we must be princes. In the world we must be kings. We must know that God made us to rule and dominate. When we rule at home, according to the word of God, we know that every other place we go will recognize our greatness. Sometimes that means we will be tempted to stray or to fight unnecessary battles because that's what happens when the world sees our obedience to Christ and sees our godly crowns.

Others are intimated by the lion because his presence alone speaks to his dominance. Each bruise and scar is a trophy he wears that tells others he defeated the last king or a predator that was threatening his land, his queen and his cubs. Each scar has its own story. He is an animal of great strength. We don't have to go around showing our battle scars because some cannot be seen. But, we have to be willing to get scarred up to protect that which God has given us to rule over and protect.

The Hebrew word for lion is strength, "Strong-one." He is the very incarnation of strength, even when dead and the skin is stripped from its body, the tremendous muscular development will create a sense of awe. The muscles of the lion are so hard that they can blunt the edge of a knife when dissected. The lion's body has terminating tendons as strong as steel. His neck muscles possess the strength as strong as the power of a crane, which enables it to lift and carry its prey, effortlessly, to a secure place.

The lion is one of the most courageous animals in existence. When the lion is driven to fight and his anger is heightened, it cares nothing about the number of foes he faces. He cares not if a hunter has a weapon when it's time to fight. When a lion or lioness is driven to fight it is the most terrible animal in existence. YOU must have that fight when it comes to what God has blessed you with.

When God made a promise to Israel in Genesis 15:18 He declared to Abraham, *"To your descendants I give this land, from the river Egypt to the great river, Euphrates,"* He also later confirmed this promise to Abraham's son, Isaac and Isaac's son, Jacob. When the Israelites were about to invade the Promised Land, God reiterated the land promise, as recoded in Joshua 1:4. *"Your territory will extend from the desert to Lebanon, and from the great river Euphrates-all the Hittite country-to the Great Sea on the west."*

The reason I'm sharing this information with you is to tell you that you'll need more space to live when you gain wisdom, grow up, and become as bold as the lion. The whole jungle belongs to the lion. You have to know this when God gives you a family to protect. You become their hedge of protection, just like the lion is the hedge of protection for his den, because you will always have people watching you who are either waiting for your demise or learning how to be the next king.

King of His Offspring

The lion is a ferocious advocate. Vacillating with fervor. Moving in strength. Loyal to his pride with surgeon-like strikes and a keen sense of the world around him. The lion is one of the most feared animals in the world. At the same time, the lion is an affectionate beast that lets his guard down among those he loves. Male lions do not look after the cubs in a pride and take no part in helping raise the young, but they do protect the whole pride against other males. The cubs are safe as long as their father is in charge of the pride. He is a husband to the pride and a father to his children. He is the king of his offspring.

Men with children can learn a great deal from a lion so they can be fully in charge of their household. The Word of God does not leave us in the dark concerning what is required of fathers with families, especially with children.

Ephesians 6:4 has a great deal to say to fathers and I'd like to spend some time sharing some valuables truths with you.

First and foremost, *fathers, do not exasperate your children*. The word, translated fathers, could very well be translated parents. It includes both the father and the mother. It is also true that the emphasis is placed largely upon the father, for he is responsible for what the children become.

Fathers, that is sobering. Is it not?

Mothers may enforce policy, but it is the father's task to set it and to see that his children are raised properly. There is nothing more dishonoring to the spirit of Christianity than the attitude adopted by many fathers: "It is my job to make the living; her job is to raise the children." That thought process is not in the Word of God. In the Bible, the ultimate responsibility for what a home becomes is the father's. So the word is addressed to fathers. This is the way a father subjects himself to his children—by deliberately avoiding the things that make a child rebel.

Do not exasperate your children.

Instead, bring them up in the training and instruction of the Lord. The word, exasperate, used here means anger that results in rebellion. Fathers, do not provoke your children to the place where they completely lose control and break out against authority. In this society and culture it is definitely easy to lose your children because the world demands that parents are obsolete. From what I know as a parent and a pastor, there are two things that cause rebellion in children: indulgence and harshness. These two things are the negatives that cause tension in the household and make the father's role difficult, at best.

A father must be able to instruct his children and be able to bring them up in the training as well as the instruction or the exhortation of the Lord. The opposites of these are indulgence and harshness. A lack of discipline will make a child insecure, miserable, and self-centered. That is what we call a spoiled child; one who grows up to expect to have his or her way in everything and who rides roughshod over the feelings of everyone else. This is created by a spirit of indulgence on the part of parents who allow their children to make decisions that no child is capable of making. And trust me, an undisciplined child becomes an undisciplined adult. This is why parents must learn that they need to make decisions for their children for quite a while in their life and only gradually help them to learn to make those decisions as they are able to do so.

The other extreme that provokes a child to revolt is harshness, rigorous, and demanding discipline that is never accompanied with love or understanding. Rigid, military discipline that says, “Do this, or this, or else,” will inevitably drive a child to revolt as he comes to adolescence. Again, a child needs to be properly led and cared for. In my generation I believe that many of us grew up with rigid parents. They probably barely showed love because they thought they were preparing us for the harsh world that was (and is at times) cruel to certain people. If you think about it, I believe this is why we as parents are more lenient towards our children.

Do you see the cycle and understand the role of you as the father?

This is why it is important to do two things when it comes to your children, training and instruction in the Lord. As a parent you have to listen to the word for instruction which is really putting your mind on the Lord. As the child grows older, physical discipline is to be replaced by exhortation and by understanding which helps a child to see what lies behind the restrictions and always shows concern and love. It does not mean a total relaxing of limits, but it means a different way of enforcing them. No matter how you were raised by your father, or if you had no male figure in the home, you can change the mistakes you have made as a parent into opportunities for advancement in your children's lives as well as your own life.

Thanks be to God for the ability to correct past mistakes.

Are we, as men, able to see and acknowledge two common behaviors that cause rebellion in our children? What training and instruction does our Father in Heaven give us?

King of His Circumstances

The lion can change any circumstance by how he roars. When he roars, there is no beast that can produce such a sound as this. There is no other animal that can be mistaken for, or compared to, a lion when he roars. The lion has a habit of stooping his head down towards the ground when he roars so the sound rolls along the ground like thunder. He is not like a thermometer that gives you the temperature, but he has the power of a thermostat … he changes the environment. He reverberates an echo up to 2.5 miles and he does this to put his enemies in a state of confusion and panic. They hear his roar, but cannot determine from which direction it is coming. It has a curious effect on the nervous system. The roar invokes fear because the hearer knows when a lion is near it is not safe. It's a feeling of mixed awe and maniacal admiration. The effect of the roar states, 'I am in charge of this territory.' It's not just a sound but it's symbolic of who he is.

Many believers think that noise is a sign of power. But the noise has no power if the fight has no impact. Men have been given the right to rule and praise God in such a way that our enemies should get confused. We are the heads after Christ and that's why when we open our mouths to praise we give a roar that makes our enemies tremble. Our praise confuses the enemy. Maybe it's because we were designed to be so closed off emotionally that when we offer our praise, and sometimes our tears, we show our strength … our roar.

Do you have anything to be thankful for?

If you do, and I know you do, then we have been given lion-like qualities and we should be the loudest and the most enthusiastic.

We all know the story of the Cowardly Lion in the classic movie "The Wizard of Oz." He overcame all kinds of threats and obstacles as he traveled down the yellow brick road with Dorothy, the Tin Man, and the Scarecrow to get to the Wizard. But before his journey started he was cowardly, despite being the king of the jungle. Everything scared him and he refused to roar because he thought he had no power in his own ability to be king. So when he was presented with the opportunity to journey towards The Emerald City to receive courage he stepped into his first courageous moment. Once he endured all the tribulations of getting to the Wizard and even defeating The Wicked Witch of the East he returned to The Emerald City and was given a medal of courage by the Wizard.

Here's the irony of that whole situation, it turns out that he already had courage; he just didn't believe in his courage or himself. After all, he was a lion, the leader of the pack, the king of the jungle. The lion didn't have to go through all that trouble to prove himself, but he did because of his doubt.

How many of us, as men, doubt our ability to lead our families, take care of our wives and still be a man? It is so easy to get caught up in the belief that we need more than the next man. To love more women. To have more things than our neighbors that we forget that we are already God's kings on this earth. We forget our roar and our place because we are always running away from who and whose we are.

Men, we are leaders and a lot like lions in this way, by nature of the primary definition of "lead" – showing the way. The very act of being a leader is a show of courage, so if we can come that far and step to the front, there's no reason we need to "go to Oz" to find and display our courage on a consistent basis. Oftentimes, we just need a little reinforcement, drawing inspiration from other leaders (and lions) to overcome our fears, and take on all the challenges, threats, obstacles, and setbacks that come our way.

Take a look at the life of King David. His example of being a king should be all the reinforcement we need. David went through so much that when he finally became king he was ready to roar like that lion to protect his people. David was a man of praise because His God was good. It was a good God who gave David victory over the lion and the bear while tending his father's sheep. It was a good God who gave David victory over Goliath. It was a good God who protected David from King Saul. It was a good God who gave David forgiveness when he committed sin.

"Oh that men would praise the Lord for his goodness and for his wonderful works!" Psalm 107.

Knowing who you are will always produce a sound from within. I echo the words of Ingrid Bergman when she said, "I was the shyest human ever invented, but I had a lion inside me that wouldn't shut up!"

I had the privilege of watching a documentary on the lion and it put things in perspective for me even when I walk through my valley of the shadow of death. It is obvious the lion had been in a vicious battle. There were thick patches of brush tangled within his mane. His face was painted by battle scars. Drops of blood were oozing from his nostrils. He couldn't fight another second if his life depended on it.

However, for the sake of his position he was ready for the next fight. He had been bruised. He had battered. He had been beaten, but he was still the king!

Men of God, you are KINGS! You have to take your position on the throne and roar. I am not saying being a dictator but you have to stand in the word and will of God. God cannot use a man who is not willing to take his rightful position in his home as king and lord. Not LORD like Jesus Christ, but ruler of his own home. Your wife's and children's lives depend on your ability to lead and guide them in the right direction. Remember I told you that the man provides the hedge of protection over the woman and children? That's what taking your position does. And I guarantee if you have the right woman (lioness) by your side, she will not have a problem with you being her king and lord.

King, you have to get into position!

CHAPTER | ELEVEN

THE WISDOM TO REST

"Obedience can only be done after you repent. If there is a need to repent, do it today and live in abundance and at the time of repentance he will roar and then you will follow."
- Hosea 11:10

Of all the undomesticated animals none is mentioned more frequently than the lion. As I have previously stated, Jesus is symbolized as a lion. He is the lion of Judah, which is the largest tribe in the house of Israel. The symbolizing of Jesus is used in the sense of controlled majestic power. This kind of power brings responsibilities and privileges. Jesus gave wonder to the world during the time He walked on the earth and He still gives wonder to believers and new followers of Christ every day. His life still astonishes most, hence the reason there is so much "What Would Jesus Do" paraphernalia out there.

I believe this is why one of the privileges of living like the lion is the right he has been given to rest. The lioness does all the hunting while the males fit the stereotype given to men by staying at home and sleeping until dinner is ready. Lions rest about 20 hours a day and spend the other four eating or helping with strategic hunting. In a sense, they have the life of kings. They eat, drink and sleep and do away with pests. This is why lions are considered the kings of the jungle. However, lions do not get to throw their weight around because of their stature alone.

While the lion might fit the stereotype of the 21st century man, it can be noted that he must have been mighty in his day to receive such a lofty position. But, the lion can't get too comfortable for fear of a challenge for position from younger stronger males. So every day, the lion must be ready to fight for the right to rest. I know today the man cannot, and does not, have that privilege to rest that long for anything. He has to get out there and take care of his family. But, when he gets home from a long day at work he is entitled to rest until dinner is cooked. Women take note if your husband is taking care of home by having a job, paying bills and buying the food… the least you can do is take care of the home internally and cook.

I know that will burn some of you 21st century wives up but it is high time you realize that the man is king and should be treated as such. But that's another book I will be writing with my wife, Mary.

What I am saying is that each one of us needs to be lion-like believers and discover who we really are. It is a discovery moment. The current stage you're in, the age you are, the burdens you bare, the crosses you carry are all discovery moments. Don't look at how bad things are, but rather how strongly you have been created.

The Hebrews speaks of a Sabbath-rest for all the people of God. On that day we are not to work, clean or cook. The Sabbath, which is sundown Friday to sundown Saturday, is a law, according to the Bible, that many of us fail to adhere to. Yes, we all have lives and all have things to do but even God rested and He chose the Sabbath to do so. So, resting is important in order to recharge and regroup. This is why the lion rests, so that when it's time for him to act he has the energy to do so.

I know there will come a day when we all will have to rest from our burdens in this life and face our Creator. We will be buried in the grave and the worms and maggots will instinctively eat our decaying bodies. The maggot will find its way into the path of a spider. The maggots will be eaten by the spider. The spider will be eaten by the lizard, the lizard will be eaten by the snake. The snakes will slither away and be spotted by a hawk, the hawk will eat the snake. The eagle will chase the hawk, kill it, and it eat. The eagle will soars to the top of the mountain to feed her young and the process will continue. The eagle will give up the hawk, the hawk will give up the snake, the snake will give up the lizard, the lizard will give up the spider. The spider will give up the maggots that ate away at my body and the life that was lived in obedience to God will be rewarded with eternal rest.

I don't want you to wait until you are in your grave to rest. I want you to rest so that you will be able to endure your race. I use to think that I will rest when I am dead. But I have quickly learned this is not the approach God wants us to have in this world. He gave us a day of rest because he knows our purpose on this earth is ever enduring and ever enduring.

When you rest, you are able to hear from God and follow the directions He has for you. Did you know if you refuse to sleep or rest you are literally sending yourself to an early grave? Your brain does not have the ability to rest and you open yourself up to sickness and illnesses. This is why it's important to rest in God so that He can recharge you and restore you.

Faith without works is dead. But your faith cannot be fully met and experienced if you are unwilling to stop and allow God to pour back into you. This is how you become wiser… by resting in God until He tells you it's time to move.

CHAPTER | TWELVE

THE WISDOM OUT OF DISOBEDIENCE

"If we hear the voice of the Lord anymore then surely we will die."
- Deuteronomy 5:25

I know I have talked a lot about the animals and what they mean and how they are obedient to what God placed inside of them. They live a life that is free of sin because of their instinctive nature to harken to what they know to be their creators voice. We came in and disrupted their normal behavior. But, let's take a moment to bring this wilderness from the wild concept to a full circle. Let's go back to Adam and Eve and how they were disrupted, and subsequently punished, for their disobedience.

What's That Sound?

Perfection fascinates me. Just to know that God planted a garden, the Garden of Eden. Can you imagine having God as a gardener? He made everything and it was beautiful and perfect. The Garden of Eden was a scene of beauty, a sunny region of delights. To this day, man has made lavish attempts to recapture God's creative genius. It is, however, questionable if any of the most skilled expositors have succeeded in reproducing the gorgeous spectacle of Eden. Have they even the understanding to reproduce the endlessly diversified assortment of lovely forms of radiant colors that seemed to comprise a narrow room of nature's wealth? Eden was described as a heaven on earth, divinely prepared by God, who caused it to spring up and bloom before the wondering eye of man.

God clothed the lilies of the field, placed rivers that freely flowed around the Garden, not requiring rainfall that provided extra beauty and water for the garden. There was so much to enjoy in this wonderful garden. God's beautiful handiwork must have covered miles and miles. Imagine, God the botanist. Certainly, if He planted it, it was a lovely and delightful place. However, even in a place so beautiful, there was one element that seemed to tarnish its beauty.

Sin.

That's what tempted His man to forsake all of the perfection of Eden. Man's disobedience was so great that it stamped judgement on us to this day. The judgment scene opens in Genesis 3 with a sound never heard by the ears of mankind. It was the sound of the Lord's coming. Let me pause for a minute and enlighten you on how much of an honor it was and is to hear the voice of God. In the Old Testament, God spoke directly to His man. Abraham, Isaac, Moses, Job all experienced the voice of God. They didn't tremble or fear His voice because they knew they had been selected for the purpose and they were living in obedience. They stumbled and God punished them but for the most part, they lived a life pleasing to God. This is why He selected them to lead. In Israel's disobedience God stopped speaking to Israel when they went into complete disobedience by following other nations. There is no account in the New Testament that He spoke to anyone, outside of Christ. Angels spoke for Him when He reached out to the disciples. That means there was a time when God was very close to man. And His closeness starts in the Garden. You can argue that God allowed man to be destroyed but He didn't. His loving heart allowed Adam to be tempted because He wanted man to experience His loving heart.

Think of it as a parent's love for their child. We warn our children but most of the time they will do what they want to do and we still have to love them. We tell them to clean up behind themselves, to make good grades, and be good people but there will come a time when they disobey and do what they want to do. Peer pressure is sometimes at the root cause of their disobedience but, for the most part, it ultimately boils down to what they want to do. Just like your child, immediately after Adam and Eve disobeyed God's command they both realized they were in trouble. God reached out to hug Adam in the place where he normally was, and Adam was no longer there. His sin put distance between him and God, requiring God to call him away from the beguiling enemy.

"Adam, where art thou?" God asked.

We all know God doesn't need to be told of our geographical location, but He wanted Adam to confess where he was. At the moment of his disobedience, Adam was no longer like God. Adam's innocence, purity, and holiness went away the reality of the world was colliding against what God told him not to do. Adam and Eve were able to differentiate between good and evil. In order to get to the root of this disobedience matter, we need to ask the right question, "How did Adam fall?"

For many years, my answer to that question was that Adam disobeyed. That seems simple enough, doesn't it? God told Adam not to eat; Adam ate. End of story.

Only it's not the end of the story. It's not even the right story. Adam's disobedience was not the problem, but rather the symptom of a deeper issue, which was that he did not trust God. In eating of the forbidden fruit, Adam declared God to be an untrustworthy liar.

Through his actions he was saying, "God, I'm better off without you."

Big mistake because distrust follows doubt.

Satan said to Eve, "Has God indeed said you shall eat of every tree of the garden?"

Satan took God positive instruction and sought to paint it as something restrictive. Eve answered correctly … almost. She said, *"You must not eat fruit from the tree that is in the middle of the garden, and YOU MUST NOT TOUCH IT or you will die."*

That was the opening Satan desired. Some of the biblical scholars state, as soon as the woman had asserted this, the serpent pushed her against the tree and said, *"See, thou hast touched it, and art still alive; thou mayest therefore safely eat of the fruit, for surely thou shalt not die."*

Could it be that Eve's addition to God's command was the handle that Satan needed? Satan declared openly that God will not do what He said. And then he sought to impugn God's character. He said, *"For God knows that when you eat of it your eyes will be opened, and you will be like God, knowing good and evil."*

Satan implied the only reason God placed the restriction on them in the first place was because He was protecting His own "turf." God was staving off the competition. You can see what Satan was banking on. It should sound familiar because Satan wanted God's turf but lost the battle when he was kicked out of heaven. So, he was using his scenario to fill the head of Eve because she wasn't created the same way Adam was created. She was made from Adam.

Let me break this down for those of you who believe that Eve was made from the dust of the ground as Adam (Gen. 2:7). She was not. God decided that His man should not be alone in Gen. 2:18 and in verse 21-25 he put man into a deep sleep and then created Eve from his rib. It is also important to know that God did make other people as you read in Gen. 1:27 but Adam was His special creation, which signifies the birth of the nation of Israel. I'll get to that later. When Satan planted his deceit with Eve he was sure they would respond by saying, "Hey, why should I be the servant? I'd rather be God."

Satan knew as long as Adam and Eve depended on God, they could not be touched. While they trusted God's promise they were under His protection. So Satan first set out to get Eve to question God's credibility, which gave him direct access to Adam, the person he was after all along. His plan to get them to move out of the protected area and into the line of fire worked because he told Eve that she should be equal to God, not obedient to Him. Once they partook in the fruit, his plan worked and it still works today. Divide us from God and conquer us with sin.

Like us, Adam lived in a world of uncertainty. Like us, he had questions he couldn't answer himself. I believe that Adam internally toiled with these questions:

- Why did God forbid me to eat from this one particular tree?
- What is this death he said would come if I eat from it?

Adam was in the dark – and that was the whole point. God purposely set things up that way because He wanted Adam and Eve to trust Him. By introducing uncertainty into their world, He was inviting them to a relationship of dependence on Him. If they had trusted God, then they would have lived blemish and pain free. They would have had an abundant life, but they chose not to trust God. So they reaped the awful consequences of their choice. It's unfortunate that people think God rejected Adam in the Garden, but it's the other way around. Adam rejected God. By spurning God's words of life he cut himself off from the source of life and when you do that you die. And that is the real story of humanity. It's a matter of trust!

I think about the many people who forfeit God's best because they fail to trust and obey Him. Distrust leads to doubt and that ultimately leads to disobedience. The problem with lacking trust in God is not that we want to sin but we doubt what God has said. At that moment you don't trust God but you put your trust in what you can see, touch, taste, hear, think. When I listen to people tell me where they are in their lives, I often wonder what happened to them that made them lose trust in God? I wonder why they don't trust Him like they trust in their loved ones, his or her spouse, their kids, their jobs, or their worldly possessions. I have to refrain from asking some of the tough questions because I know the frailty of the human condition and my job as a pastor is to lead the flock back to God, not away.

The Sound of Doom

There was a sound I hated to hear when growing up.

"Patrick James Diggs! Do you hear me calling you?"

As a young boy when my mother called the entire name that is printed on my birth certificate, it usually meant trouble for me. Something serious was about to go down, usually, on my backside. This is where the leather met my Levis. But nevertheless, to call me by my birth name carried a sound that unfortunately meant her patience had worn thin and her presence was fast approaching.

This was the sound of judgment.

The voice of my mother or my father thundering through the house was enough to stop all activities until whatever was wrong was corrected. Just like when you have erred or not kept the commandments the voice of God is no longer calm or a sound of harmony but a thundering roar. It is usually because we have disobeyed a direct order from God. If you pay close attention while reading Genesis 3:8 you can hear the conversation that Adam and Eve had behind the bushes after the forbidden fruit was tasted.

"Shhhhh! Be quiet! The Lord is coming…" said Adam to Eve.

"Why? Are we not His equal? We have eaten from the tree so now we are just like Him," Eve responded.

"No, we are just like Him," he responds. "We were disobedient and now we must hide because He will see our guilt and know that we are no longer how He made us."

Unfortunately, there is no place you can hide from God. David reminds us that the presence of the Lord passes Himself from the east to west. He can look at the past, standing in the present, while watching events unfold in the future. What a mighty God He is! Adam and Eve felt a presence more powerful than they've ever felt before. This is the sound of judgment. They'd never heard such rumbling before. The sound of God's voice alone caused Adam and Eve to retreat into the bushes. Something I am sure they never experienced before but, because they were filled with fear, they fled to cover.

This is how you know when you're in a place of disobedience. When God shows up and you're happy about the visit but instead you are in fear of judgment. Adam and Eve tried to cover their guilt and shame from God, but they chose a poor cover up. Fig leaves. God, however, chose skins to cover Adam and Eve in Genesis 3:21, *"And the Lord God made garments of skin for Adam and his wife, and clothed them."*

Manmade solutions for sin and guilt never work. Fig leaves of religious works will never cover the guilty sinner nor will it make him right with God. Sin always makes a report to your conscience. It reports, "You are naked." "Hide here come God."

Adam and Eve participated in the classic game of hide and seek by covering themselves up. This is a visual of our fruitless efforts to cover our guilty souls. Now, there's a sense of shame and a conscious filled with guilt. Adam and Eve felt as if they had fallen because the taste of death was still on their lips. It is impossible to sin and not feel as though you've lost some purity. Adam and Eve were naked. They had always been naked, but now they were aware and ashamed of it. What an uncomfortable feeling that was. They were hiding their bodies because the temptation to satisfy the flesh was the root of the problem. They felt defenseless, vulnerable and exposed.

Sin makes you feel that way ... naked. Only human beings feel naked. We are the only creatures God made who cover our bodies. First, we used fig leaves stitched together but today our clothing is more sophisticated. Ralph Lauren dresses and Armani suits. Costly, yes, but no different from fig leaves in purpose. And costly is what happened when disobedience entered into the Garden. We covered our guilt then and we do it today. Yes, with clothes but with other sins like sexual immorality, drugs and alcohol abuse, lies, deception, murder, adultery, and so many other sins, just to mask the sin of disobedience.

Things We Hide From

Are you like Adam and Eve? Living every moment of your life in hiding? Are you running from God so much that you hide yourself from Him at every turn? You hide behind fig leaves of public image. You hide behind your work. You hide by always being busy and doing things that you know you are not supposed to be doing. You hide behind the drugs, the alcohol. You hide from reality. People will hide behind social standing, behind educational degrees, and behind church. They hide behind these things because they don't want to be naked before God. However, sin leaves you naked even if you are fully clothed. We cover up our sins by telling ourselves they are not so bad.

"Look at everybody else. They are all doing it," are the words we use to justify our wrongdoings against God.

We also hide from each other, from offering understanding, love, and a helping hand. We hide because we do not want to get involved. We do not love. When we are angry, we hide behind anonymous letters, social media posts, behind grumbling, gossip, and complaining. You hide behind all of these things because you feel naked, as a result of sin. Like Adam and Eve, you crouch down in the bushes when God is trying to fellowship with you. We blatantly disobey His word which reaches beyond the boundaries of our understanding. We think we know who we are but we don't want to be that person because that person requires that we keep up with and follow the commandments, laws, and statues set by God throughout the entire Bible. We refuse to be completely bold in obedience so we settle on being disobedient. As God is trying to draw nearer to us we run and hide from Him. But here's a newsflash God always knows where you are. This is why we always have questions about our relationship with God and the purpose of our lives.

Where are you with respect to Him? With respect to your wife/husband? With respect to the creation of which you are a part?

God calls out to us in our hiding places. He will not leave us alone. *"Where are you?"* He says.

He calls to us in our hiding places, in our work cubicles, in our cars, at our dining room tables, and in our beds.

"Where are you?" He asks.

He calls to us in our relationships, in our singleness, in our marriages.

"Where are you?" He asks.

In the adversities we face, the disease, the rebellious son or daughter, in the fire and tornado God is calling to us.

"Where are you?" He asks.

Exposed, Adam hides behind excuses. "I heard you in the garden, but I was afraid because I was naked, so I hid."

God said, *"Who said you were naked?"*

The real problem wasn't Adam being naked. God made him that way. The problem was Adam's disobedience. Adam ate of knowledge and was immediately introduced to death. He became an enemy of God. Fear and shame were his problem, not God's. As an enemy, he could flee God or fight Him. What's your excuse? Why are you hiding from God? Why don't you have a greater desire to hear from God, to listen to His voice in Scripture, to pray to Him for hours each day as you would talk to a dear friend? What is your excuse? Business? Family? Work? Life? Other plans? Why is God not important to you?

The answer to our hiding is confession. We speak to God and admit our shame. Adam and Eve didn't confess. They pointed fingers at each other. Adam said the woman made me do it. Eve said the serpent made her do it. But, in reality, they did it because they no longer trusted that

God was who He said He was. They took a leadership role they were not equipped or prepared for. We do that when we rush to make decisions without consulting and waiting on God. We allow ourselves to become Godlike when we handle our problems on our own. We also take a bite of the forbidden fruit daily. That's why when we go against God's will and disobey Him we must subject ourselves to confession.

Confession, which is repentance, draws us out of hiding. We reveal ourselves to God. He knows our hearts before we speak, but confession admits it to God. We have to confess that we are by nature sinful and unclean. We have to confess that we have sinned against God by word and deed. Confession is a kind of death. We die to our self-delusion that we can cover our sins and hide from God. When we confess our sins and say to God, "Here I am. Yes, I'm a sinner please help me for the sake of your Son Jesus." God is then able to do His part. Our confession becomes our repentance.

The secret to life is not "obey or die" it's "trust God or die trying." (See John 5:24 and 11:25)

The bottom line is not whether you obey God but whether you trust Him. It is impossible to trust God and not obey Him, but there are plenty of people who think they are obeying God yet they don't trust Him. These people sin carelessly and live presumptuously. They believe, as long as they say their prayers, accept Christ as Savior, go to church regularly, or do a good deed here and there, that they are alright. They sin as if there are no consequences. You know these people. You may be one of these people who believe that going to church on a regular basis, saying your prayers day in and day out, giving a tithe is what will get you into the kingdom. It's not. You have to keep God's commandments, which is simply obeying Him. It is hard. It is a struggle but do you want to constantly ask yourself, "What was the sound? Was it His voice? Was it His footsteps?" as He is passing you to restore and reward those who work diligently to remain obedient to Him.

Those questions can be answered like this... That sound is the sound of doom, disruption, and the sound that destroys your relationship with God. When you live in disobedience you disrupt your ability to feel the presence of God. Your disobedience causes disorder and chaos in a place where there was once contentment and peaceful pleasure. Just remember this ... God will never give you something that requires you to disobey Him, in order to keep it.

A life of obedience always sounds like the hymn every believer should remember. *"Amazing grace how sweet the sound that saved a wretch like me I once was lost but now I'm found 'twas blind but now I see…"*

Unfortunately, the world has tainted our listening, hearing and believing and we fail to see the simplest request from God. Obedience. We have allowed society to define what obedience is for us. We believe more in the laws of the land and the popular trending societal standards that we give up our salvation and peace. We trade faith for fads. We trade hope for hype. We trade trust in God for trust in man. It's time for us to hear that sound and know that is God who wants us to be in His presence. He wants for us to return to Him and to that place of rest. Not as a last resort but as the only place.

Obedience is powerful.

ABOUT THE AUTHOR

Patrick J. Diggs is a native of Fort Worth, TX January 10, 1972. He attended schools in Fort Worth Public Schools. He announced his call to preach in 2000 and has been the lead pastor of New Fellowship since 2008 with an active membership of more than 400 members. Diggs life's journey as a pastor would change considerably when he answered God's instructions to build the new facility for New Fellowship on June 1, 2008. Even with very limited funds and membership, God used the faith of a few followers and in November of 2011, along with new members, the doors of New Fellowship opened for its first worship service. Diggs believes in his calling and understands that it takes strong faith as well as a strong church to build strong families.

Diggs works tirelessly and diligently to teach men their God ordained role at home as well as helping them understand the works to get them to become more involved in church to make sure their lives are guided by practical Christian principles. The mission of New Fellowship Church of Fort Worth is to live for Jesus, look for the lost, and love others with the love of Christ.

Diggs is currently enrolled in Southwestern Baptist Theological Seminary and also serves on the JPS Pastoral Council, a Campus Coach for Read2Win, and actively involved the Fort Worth community. He is also a certified fitness instructor and in 2014 he released his first workout video entitled Temple XII Fitness. He is continuously revolutionizing ministry by helping his members, as well as other, get spiritually in tuned as well as physically.

Diggs is married to Mary Diggs and has four children Jordan, Britney, Raven, and James Diggs.

www.ingramcontent.com/pod-product-compliance
Lightning Source LLC
La Vergne TN
LVHW051233080426
835513LV00016B/1552
9780692497258